THE HEART OF

By the same author:

The Heart of Revival

NICKY GUMBEL

KINGSWAY PUBLICATIONS
EASTBOURNE

Co-published in South Africa with SCB Publishers
Cornelis Struik House, 80 McKenzie Street
Cape Town 8001, South Africa.
Reg no 04/0203/06

Text illustrations by Charlie Mackesy

ISBN 0 85476 756 8

Designed and produced by Bookprint Creative Services
P.O. Box 827, BN21 3YJ, England, for
KINGSWAY PUBLICATIONS
Lottbridge Drove, Eastbourne, East Sussex BN23 6NT.
Printed in Great Britain.

Contents

Foreword

'Will you not revive us again, that your people may rejoice in you?' was the cry of the psalmist (Ps 85:6). And it is the cry of the church once again. As so many dreadful things are hurled into our consciousness every day, through the media and our own observation or experience, there is a growing hunger in many hearts for God to do something radical, exciting, real and new.

There are, of course, many encouraging signs. Churches all over the world are beginning to see shoots of new life springing up, sometimes in unlikely settings. Alpha courses (Alpha is a fifteen-session practical introduction to the Christian faith) are growing in churches, homes and prisons; the spiritual atmosphere is softer in many ways than it has been in our time before.

Against this encouraging background it is not surprising that there is so much discussion today about revival. Churches and intercessory groups are praying for, believing for and expecting revival. Some people are understandably confused. What do we do while we are waiting for revival? Is there life before revival? How do we recognise it and are we seeing something of it now—or not?

History shows that when revival comes men and women come alive to the life of God. Indeed, one definition might be 'to wake up and live'. It involves breathing—as the fundamental expression of life—breathing in God's Spirit and breathing out his love for the church and, through the church, the world.

In 1953 Edwin Orr, the Irish evangelist and revival historian, prophesied that the Holy Spirit was beginning to raise up a new generation of revived leaders who would be used to support and sustain a programme of revival and co-operative evangelism. Whatever he meant exactly, Nicky Gumbel is clearly one of those he was speaking about.

Nicky's approach to this whole subject is refreshingly well researched and informed. Interpreting some of the teaching in the book of Isaiah he draws out important truths for today, steering away from the hazards of speculative enthusiasms to produce a well-balanced and immensely readable study. His own positive style and Charlie Mackesy's delightful illustrations make this an ideal book for any who want to find out more about this important subject. Whether you have just graduated from Alpha, or have been a Christian for some years, I am confident that *The Heart of Revival* will not only give you a fresh hunger and expectation for revival but also a proper understanding of what it might mean and how you can prepare. I commend it to you.

Sandy Millar
Holy Trinity Brompton

Preface

The purpose of this book is to look at the text of Isaiah 40–66 and to see what lessons can be learned for today's church. Of course, there is a great deal of difference between our modern use of the word 'revival' and the issues that form the background to these chapters in Isaiah. Nevertheless, there are many similarities and strong links between the two and it is these that I have sought to examine in this book.

One of the ways I hope the book might be used is as study material for small groups. We have already produced a number of follow-up books to Alpha but this is the first one that covers Old Testament material. I hope some will find it a helpful way to start studying the Old Testament.

The book has been a team effort and I am very grateful to those who have given their valuable time, energy and skills to helping with the project. In particular I would like to thank Preb. John Collins, Preb. Sandy Millar, the Very Revd Dr Tom Wright, the Revd Dr David Stone, Dr Peter Somers Heslam, Zilla Hawkins, Jo Glen, Helena Hird, Dr Roland Werner, Si Levell, the Revd Chris Russell, Annie Sutherland, Sue Arundale, Andrew Brydon, Chris Smith, and the

Revd Jon Soper. As always, the imperfections and mistakes are my own responsibility. Finally, my thanks to Philippa Pearson Miles, Katie Mason and Juliet Sloggett for their great efficiency and patience in dealing with the numerous drafts, redrafts, changes and corrections over the past three years.

1

What Is Revival?

Introduction to Isaiah 40–66

Revival, um, I think it's a type of drink.

I have often wondered what 'revival' would look like. In Hyde Park on Saturday 6 September 1997 I saw thousands upon thousands of people moving in a quiet and unobtrusive way in one direction. There was a sense of being united in love, perhaps even of repentance and a desire to see a more compassionate world. The crowds were moving towards two vast screens where they were going to participate in a service of Christian worship in which they would be joined via satellite by 2,500 million people, almost half of humanity. The occasion was, of course, the funeral of Diana, Princess of Wales.

Millions prayed together, asking that God's name would be honoured, that his kingdom would come, and that his will would be done on earth as it is in heaven. Prayers were led in the name of Jesus. It occurred to me as we prayed that perhaps this could be a glimpse of what 'revival' might look like were the sadness of that occasion to be replaced with joy.

From time to time, we hear reports of revival from various parts of the world. A man once introduced himself to me in the bookshop at our church. His name was Dr Cheung. He is the Director of Evangelism for Dr David Yonggi Cho, pastor of the Full Gospel Central Church in Seoul, the capital of South Korea. I asked Dr Cheung how many home groups he had in that congregation. He replied, '50,000.' 'How many members do you have?' I asked. He replied, '750,000.' In 1961 they had 600 members. By the beginning of 1980 they had 100,000 members. It is now the largest church in the world. Seoul is the home of ten of the twenty largest congregations in the world.

In 1845 the first missionaries arrived in Korea. In 1866 Robert Thomas, a Welshman serving in China as a missionary, went to Korea to distribute Bibles among the Chinese-speaking people there. On arrival his ship was given a hostile reception: as it came close to land Korean soldiers attacked it and threw burning brands on to the deck. The crew were forced to abandon the burning vessel and many died. Robert Thomas gathered some of his Bibles and began to wade through the shallow water to land. On the shore he was savagely attacked, but he pressed his Bibles into the hands of his murderers before he collapsed and died. 'And so the soil of North Korea drank the blood of a martyr on the very same spot where forty years later, the revival took place.'[1]

In 1900 there were only 50,000 Christians in Korea. In spite of communist persecution 'revival' broke out in Pyongyang in 1907. Over the next ten years church membership quadrupled. By 1990 there were 12 million Christians in South Korea (Seoul was 40 per cent Christians and had more than 7,000 churches). Over twenty churches are planted every day and the gospel has penetrated every part of society. Every morning at 5am about one million South Korean Christians pray for their country and for revival to spread throughout Asia and the rest of the world.

'Revival' is also taking place in China. *Asia Week*, in an article 'The Great Awakening—China's Christian Revival' reported what it described as 'one of the most dramatic revivals in the history of Christianity'. In 1950, there were officially fewer than 4 million Christians in China. In 1977, the Communist party view was this: 'We believe that all religion is superstition, impeding the Revolution. There are probably a few Christians left but they are all old. They will die off and that will be the end of it.' Yet today Christianity is flourishing in China as never before, with some reports indicating growth of 25,000 per day. Dr Hudson Taylor III (grandson of the nineteenth-century missionary to China) says, 'The Chinese experience is eloquent testimony that no earthly force can eliminate God's power. Truth burns brightest where the fire burns hottest.'[2]

In April 1994 *The Guardian* newspaper reported that 'Christian fever' is sweeping China, evidenced by vast meetings (even at night), mass baptisms and miracles of healing. One pastor comments that 'going to South Henan is akin to stepping back into the pages of the Acts of the Apostles and first-century Christianity. Almost every village is aflame with revival fires . . . Thousands, predominantly young people, are converting to the faith. Many will tell you about answers to prayer, miracles, deliverance.'[3]

Likewise, Argentina has seen extraordinary 'revival' in recent times, one example being the work of Carlos Anacondia, a businessman and lay preacher. He held a three-month crusade in La Plata where it was reported that 40,000 made public professions of faith in Christ. Next, he moved on to Mar del Plata where 90,000 'decisions' were reported, followed by a further 70,000 in San Justo. From then on, city after city was stirred by his ministry with large numbers being converted at his rallies, together with many exorcisms and healings. It is now estimated that Anacondia has led over 2 million to Christ.[4] For the last thirteen years the 'revival' has continued. Thousands of churches have been planted, sometimes in old theatres and disused cinemas. Some of the larger churches hold several services each day.

The Olmos prison, in Buenos Aires, is the largest maximum security prison in Argentina. It is also the home of the largest prison church in the world. 'Revival' has broken out and has transformed not only the lives of thousands of inmates and their families but also the prison itself. Olmos once had a well-deserved reputation for violence and terror: black magic and violent crime were everyday occurrences. Christians were scarce and were not welcomed by inmates or prison officials.

Then, in 1988, 'revival' began. Today the Olmos church has more than 1,200 members, 40 per cent of the prison population. Their radical lifestyle is a challenge to Christians everywhere. Six days a week meetings are held with praise, worship, prayer and preaching. Since the church has established itself in the prison, violence has diminished dramatically. A favourite saying among the inmates is, 'Neither my mother, nor electric shock torture, nor beating by the police could change my life. Only Jesus could do that!'

In Brazil churches are growing as never before. Brazil for Christ Church, San Paulo, is led by Manoel de Melo. Since 1955 they have planted 6,000 churches, 1,000 in San Paulo alone. The 'mother' church has 25,000 members. In total there are 1.2 million members as a result of plants from that church.[5] One minister writes, 'We are living in a revival . . . more than 30 per cent [of Brazilians] now confess Jesus as Lord.'[6]

There are also signs of 'revival' in North America. *The New York Times* reported on what is happening in Pensacola, Florida: 'Revivals come and go, but what has been happening here for almost two years is different. What started as a typical temporary revival on Father's Day 1995 has snowballed into what is apparently the largest and longest Pentecostal revival in America in almost a century.'[7] Over 100,000 have come to Christ.

As we read of such accounts we long to see 'revival' in our church and nation. But what do we mean by the word 'revival'?

The Old Testament word for 'revive' comes from a word meaning 'to live', which originally conveyed the idea of breathing. Altogether this word is used in its various forms more than 250 times in the Old Testament. It may be translated as 'revive', 'live', 'restore', 'preserve', 'heal', 'prosper', 'flourish', 'save', or some other similar term. The comparable New Testament word means 'to live again'.

In church history the word 'revival' has been variously defined. In North America it was understood to refer to 'some special seasons wherein God doth in a remarkable manner revive religion among his people'.[8] Jonathan Edwards, the eighteenth-century theologian and preacher, used it to describe a 'surprising work of God' and explained it as 'God's major means of extending his kingdom'. The writer on revivals, Edwin Orr, defined revival as 'a movement of the Holy Spirit bringing about a revival of New Testament Christianity in the church of Christ and its related community'. Later it came to be used instead of the word 'mission' or 'campaign'. Some make the distinction between 'revival' as a sovereign act of God and 'revivalism' which is seen in terms of an organised event or campaign.[9]

The word 'revival' has often been displaced by words like 'reform', 'renewal', 'restoration', or 'a time of refreshing'. Yet another term is 'awakening'. Edwin Orr commented that, 'The logic of words suggests "revival" for the revitalising of a body of Christian believers, and "awakening" for the stirring of interest in the Christian faith in the related community of nominal Christians or unbelievers.' The Oxford Association for Research in Revival has adopted 'revival' for believers, and 'awakening' for the wider community.

Of course, the meaning of a word is determined by its usage. There is nothing wrong with any of these ways of defining revival. In this book we are using it in the widest possible sense of the word, to include renewal, restoration, refreshing and awakening. Author Brian Edwards wrote, '"Revival" swallows up all other words as the shark swallows the shrimp.'[10]

Perhaps one of the best definitions is the one used by Duncan Campbell, who was himself involved in the 1949 revival in the Hebrides. He described revival as 'a community saturated with God'.

On the Day of Pentecost a group of believers became 'a community saturated with God'. Author and church leader John Stott, commenting on Acts chapter 2, writes:

> Pentecost has been called—and rightly—the first 'revival', using this word to denote one of those unusual visitations of God, in which a whole community becomes vividly aware of his immediate, overpowering presence. It may be, therefore, that not only the physical phenomena (vv. 2 ff.), but the deep conviction of sin (v. 37), the 3,000 conversions (v. 41) and the widespread sense of awe (v. 43) were signs of 'revival'. We must be careful, however, not to use this possibility as an excuse to lower our expectations, or to relegate to the category of the exceptional what God may intend to be the church's normal experience.[11]

Revival involves more than personal renewal. As individuals come alive to the reality of Christ, and this experience is multiplied in the lives of others, the church feels a new unity of faith and purpose. As hearts are filled with the love of Christ, the dynamic for a compelling evangelism is born. Society inevitably feels the impact of this renewal. Restitutions are made. Broken homes are reunited. Public moral standards improve. Integrity makes its way into government. Robert E. Coleman, Director of Wheaton

College, Illinois (which experienced an extraordinary move of God's Spirit in 1995), observes that 'to the extent that the spirit of revival prevails, mercy, justice and righteousness sweep over the land'.[12]

In the text of Isaiah 40–66 we find many themes that relate to the subject of revival and an essential message from God which is as relevant to us today as it was to the people of Israel hundreds of years ago. In order to see why, we need to look at the background to these chapters.

The book of Isaiah has been described as 'the Bible in miniature'. There are sixty-six books of the Bible. There are sixty-six chapters in our modern version of Isaiah. As the Bible is divided into two Testaments, so may Isaiah be divided into two parts. There are thirty-nine books in the Old Testament and thirty-nine chapters in the first part of Isaiah. Likewise, there are twenty-seven books in the New Testament and twenty-seven chapters in the second part of Isaiah. Whereas chapters 1–39 cover many of the themes of the Old Testament, chapters 40–66 cover many of those of the New Testament. These later chapters are, in fact, rather like sunshine after storm clouds—full of hope, comfort and deliverance. Chapters 40–55 have even been described as 'the gospel in the Old Testament', and 'good news for ancient man'. The book of Isaiah is sometimes known as the fifth gospel. One Baptist minister, in describing how he had been brought up with this perception of Isaiah, said, 'If the other four ever got lost, it would not matter as long as we still have Isaiah.'[13]

The second part of Isaiah begins with words which are quoted later by John the Baptist (40:3). There are four so-called 'servant songs' in this section and also four gospels in the New Testament. The climax of the

book is the death and a glimpse of the resurrection of
the Servant of God (ch. 53). There follows the outpouring of the Holy Spirit (ch. 61) and a concluding
description of the new heaven and the new earth (chs
65–66). All these themes are taken up later in the New
Testament.

Hence, the material in chapters 40–66 is crucial to
our understanding of the New Testament. Jesus had a
comprehensive knowledge of the Old Testament
scriptures. These particular chapters form part of the
basis of Jesus' self-understanding of his identity and
his mission (see, for example, Luke 4:16–21).

Therefore, despite being written hundreds of years
before Jesus' birth, these passages are exciting,
encouraging and relevant for us today. The context
of the previous thirty-nine chapters is the eighth century BC, ending with the defeat of Sennacherib, King
of Assyria, at the time when his country was the
dominant world power. However, from chapter 40,
Babylon is the dominant world power and we seem to
be in the sixth century BC (the age of Confucius,
Zoroaster and Buddha). The prophet is no longer
based in Jerusalem, but among the people of God,
in exile in Babylon.[14]

Babylonia is the region of modern-day Southern
Iraq. Babylon was the political and religious capital
of Babylonia and its empire, fifty miles south of where
Baghdad is today. In 605 BC the Babylonian empire
took control of Israel and after a failed Jewish rebellion, Jerusalem fell on 16 March 597 BC. In a series of
deportations thousands of Israelites were taken prisoner, and Zedekiah the king had his eyes gouged out
and was put in chains and taken to Babylon. There
followed also widespread destruction of buildings,
including the spiritual and cultural heart of the

nation—the temple. Israel was left humiliated, frustrated, depressed, bewildered and desolate.

It is into this situation that the prophet speaks. The message of Isaiah 40–55 is this: 'The exile will be over soon.' After decades of suffering, Babylon would be conquered by Cyrus, King of Persia, who would allow God's people to go back to Jerusalem to rebuild their city: a 'second exodus'.

The message of exile and restoration is of great relevance to us today. The words of Paul in the opening chapter of Romans are an apt description of what appears to be happening in much of today's world.

> For although they knew God, they neither glorified him as God nor gave thanks to him, but their thinking became futile and their foolish hearts were darkened. Although they claimed to be wise, they became fools and exchanged the glory of the immortal God for images made to look like mortal man and birds and animals and reptiles. Therefore God gave them over in the sinful desires of their hearts to sexual impurity for the degrading of their bodies with one another. They exchanged the truth of God for a lie, and worshipped and served created things rather than the Creator (Rom 1:21–25).

Ever since the Fall in the Garden of Eden, human beings have been in spiritual 'exile'. All of us have sinned and need a saviour. The Bible reveals that through Jesus, God seeks to deliver us from captivity to sin and to bring us to freedom. In a more specific sense, modern Western culture is undergoing a kind of 'exilic experience'. Our society has attempted to shut God out, and in many ways has succeeded, with disastrous results.

For example, every day in Britain at least:

20 schoolgirls become pregnant, 2 under the age of 13

470 babies are murdered by abortion
17 women are raped
65 per cent of videos for sale or hire deal with the occult, sex or violence
520 couples are divorced
75 children are added to child protection registers
90 children are taken into local authority care
280 children run away from home or care
150 people are found guilty by a court for drug offences

One new crime is committed every six seconds. There are two burglaries and three car crimes every sixty seconds. A violent attack takes place every two minutes. Somebody calls the Samaritans every two minutes. The United Kingdom has a higher number in prison per head of population than any other EU country. One in three under-14s admits to regular sexual intercourse. At least one person sleeping rough in London dies each week. The pornographic industry in the UK is worth over £100 million annually. Crime costs British businesses more than £5 billion per year. There are 30,000 Christian clergy of all types, but more than 80,000 registered witches and fortune tellers.[15]

These statistics are symptoms of an 'exile' from God. The theologian and writer, Tom Wright, explains the idea of 'exile' in the light of the fact that as recently as twenty years ago many people grew up in a 'church environment', knowing basic Bible stories, attending Sunday school and going to church services regularly:

Now it is totally commonplace for people in the West not to give God a thought. 'Jesus' is only a swear word. As a result—and you can plot this politically, artistically, economically and in all sorts of other ways—we are, as a culture, sliding towards exile.

When Jesus came, he was proclaiming the real end of exile. The first-century Jews knew perfectly well that all the great prophecies from Isaiah, Jeremiah, Ezekiel and others had not yet been fulfilled. The temple had not been rebuilt as it was supposed to have been. All those wonderful things that were supposed to happen, like getting rid of pagan oppressors, had not happened. So they believed that they were still in exile, and when Jesus came, it was to announce that at last, the long night of exile was over, and God was being faithful to the covenant.[16]

Although Jesus has made it possible for all people and nations to leave the sin which holds them as slaves, sin can still take an unrepentant nation or culture back into an exilic period. As the Western world has been going through such a period, many Christians have been going back to these chapters. We will not study every chapter in detail, but we will take a selection from which much can be gleaned, even hundreds of years after they were written. Here we find pointers to the answers to many of the questions people are asking about 'revival' today.

2

Is Revival Coming?

Isaiah 40

In the last few years numerous books and articles have been written on the subject of revival. Some are suggesting that we are already in revival; some that we are on the brink of revival; and still others that we are nowhere near revival. The headline in a recent edition of *The Guardian* read, 'Crisis in the Church'. There followed a sub-heading, 'Dramatic Decline in Attendance'. The article began: 'The Church of England was dealt a sharp blow yesterday when new figures revealed the biggest annual drop in the number of people attending Sunday services for 20 years and painted a grim picture of decline across the board.'[17]

On the same day, the headline in *The Church Times* was, 'Church attendance figures fall again'.[18] They showed a diagram of the fall in Sunday attendance since 1989 which made depressing reading. In the light of such headlines and articles it is easy to become discouraged and feel helpless. Where does the truth lie? Has revival come? Is revival coming? Is revival something we can plan and bring about by human efforts? Or is it something only God can initiate? If so, are we mere spectators, or are we called to respond in some way?

Lord, re. dates for revival we really feel that the 12th of June is fine

Isaiah chapter 40 begins with four voices proclaiming messages. The voices invite us to lift up our eyes and see what God is doing and what he is about to do. We are asked to stop looking down at our problems and to look up at God.

Look, it is over (vv. 1–2)

Comfort, comfort my people, says your God. Speak tenderly to Jerusalem, and proclaim to her that her hard service has been completed, that her sin has been paid for, that she has received from the Lord's hand double for all her sins.

Many people today have made a mess of their lives and would love the opportunity to make a new start. The first voice proclaims in effect, 'Look, the grim past is over.'

This is the language of marriage and of God's covenant promise to his people. It is 'your God' who speaks, and he speaks to 'my people'. The repetition of the word 'comfort' suggests emotional intensity. The Hebrew word for 'says' means 'keeps saying'. God is speaking as a lover, wooing his people and speaking to their hearts.

The Israelites were not in exile because God's power was limited, nor because the Babylonian gods were stronger than the God of Israel. The exile was caused by sin—just as sin has caused exile from the presence of God in modern Western society. Now God proclaims to Israel that 'her hard service' is over. The word for 'hard service' is the same word as for military conscription. God has, in effect, now made it possible for them to be 'demobilised'.

The same is true for us. We need no longer be conscripts, wearing the drab uniform handed out to us in the old sinful culture of exile, where we were banished from God's kingdom. Later, in chapters 52 and 53, the prophet explains how, for individuals and for a society at large, new clothes will be issued, and a new life made possible.

Look, God is coming (vv. 3–5)

A voice of one calling: 'In the desert prepare the way for the Lord; make straight in the wilderness a highway for our God. Every valley shall be raised up, every mountain and hill made low; the rough ground shall become level, the rugged places a plain. And the glory of the Lord will be revealed, and all mankind together will see it. For the mouth of the Lord has spoken.'

Within every human being there is a longing for God. Paul Johnson, writing in the *Daily Mail* on Saturday 6 September 1997, one week after Princess Diana's death, said:

> The surge of feeling for Diana this week has been a spontaneous, collective, religious act of the nation. It is a plea. Give us a spiritual dimension. Make our lives meaningful. Show us there is more to existence than getting and spending and earning and acquiring.

Deep down, consciously or unconsciously, we all long to experience the presence of God. The second voice cries out, 'Look, God is coming.'

It declares that the king is coming to his people. In many parts of the world, people prepare for a royal visitor by building roads, flattening the bumps and filling in the potholes. When God comes, valleys will be filled in and mountains will be flattened. The whole of creation will sing for joy. Mark quotes this verse at the beginning of his gospel. Here, the messenger who will prepare the way for the King is John the Baptist. 'Our God' is now 'the Lord', by whom Mark means Jesus Christ. In Isaiah 40:5, the voice proclaims that 'the glory of the Lord will be revealed'. John tells us in his gospel that the glory of the Lord is revealed in Jesus, 'who came from the Father, full of grace and truth' (Jn 1:14). This second voice promises God's presence with his people.

Look at God's word (vv. 6–8)

A voice says, 'Cry out.' And I said, 'What shall I cry?' 'All men are like grass, and all their glory is like the flowers of the field. The grass withers and the flowers fall, because the breath of the Lord blows on them. Surely the people are grass. The grass withers and the flowers fall, but the word of our God stands for ever.'

There is a quest for permanence in every human heart. When a friend dies we are reminded forcibly of the fragility of life. Is anything permanent? Yes, the prophet replies, there is something permanent. The third voice urges us, 'Look at God's word.'

After thirty-eight years in slavery, Israel's leaders had died and a whole new generation had been born in exile. They were aware of the transience of their lives and culture. They were in desperate need of a more permanent, secure, worthwhile basis for their existence as a people.

Likewise today, a generation is growing up deprived of cultural security. There is widespread cynicism about the power of any authority structure or institution to offer meaning or purpose to our lives.

However, rather than live with this insecurity exposed on the surface, many people hide it away and cling on to their money, to their image in society, to their property, or their health. But these things pass away. So God points out to his people the futility of building lives on transient, and therefore ultimately unsatisfactory, foundations.

'The word of our God,' says the voice, 'stands for ever.' Voltaire, the eighteenth-century critic of Christianity, wrote that within a hundred years the Bible would be obsolete and would have gone out of circulation altogether. Within one hundred years of his death, his own Parisian residence had been converted into a Bible depot, publishing Bibles by the hour.

Today, there is a new hunger for Jesus and more Bibles are being sold than ever before.

Jonathan Edwards, writing in 1741 and listing five distinguishing marks of the Holy Spirit's work in revival, said, 'The Spirit that operates in such a manner as to cause in men a greater regard to the Holy Scriptures, and establishes them more in their truth and divinity, is certainly the Spirit of God.'[19]

Look at God (vv. 9–11)

You who bring good tidings to Zion, go up on a high mountain. You who bring good tidings to Jerusalem, lift up your voice with a shout, lift it up, do not be afraid; say to the towns of Judah, 'Here is your God!' See, the Sovereign Lord comes with power, and his arm rules for him. See, his reward is with him, and his recompense accompanies him. He tends his flock like a shepherd: He gathers the lambs in his arms and carries them close to his heart; he gently leads those that have young.

How is such a new start possible? How can we know the presence of the Lord? How do we hear the word of the Lord? The prophet points to the only answer. The fourth voice simply says, 'Look at God.'

The voice proclaims, 'Behold your God' (RSV). He is powerful and transcendent. He rules, rewards and recompenses (v. 10). He is also an immanent God, close to his people and he is gentle, as tender as a shepherd (v. 11). He is a God of mercy. It is in the cross of Christ that we see most clearly how these two characteristics of justice and love come together.

The prophet now goes on to examine these themes in more depth. First, he explores who God is and what he wants to do in his world and with his people.

We understand more of who God is by looking in five different places.

Look at creation (vv. 12–14)

Who has measured the waters in the hollow of his hand, or with the breadth of his hand marked off the heavens? Who has held the dust of the earth in a basket, or weighed the mountains on the scales and the hills in a balance? Who has understood the mind of the Lord, or instructed him as his counsellor? Whom did the Lord consult to enlighten him, and who taught him the right way? Who was it that taught him knowledge or showed him the path of understanding?

Our God is the 'maker of heaven and earth', as the Apostles' Creed puts it. God is not part of creation, as some New Age mysticism teaches, but distinct from it. He holds the oceans in the 'hollow of his hand'. He weighs the mountains on scales. The world he made is extraordinary in its beauty, intricacy and variety. For example, there are 300,000 species of beetles and weevils alone. In one cubic foot of snow there are 18 million different snow flakes. No two human beings have the same set of fingerprints. As the poet William Blake contemplated the greatness of God he wrote that this enabled him

> To see a World in a Grain of Sand,
> And a Heaven in a Wild Flower,
> Hold Infinity in the palm of your hand,
> And Eternity in an hour.[20]

As we look at a world in which, on the whole, people know less and less about more and more, we have to stand back and marvel that God invented it, created it, sustains it and carries it forward to its final destiny. 'Behold your God!'

Look at the nations (vv. 15–17)

Surely the nations are like a drop in a bucket; they are regarded as dust on the scales; he weighs the islands as though they were fine dust. Lebanon is not sufficient for altar fires, nor its animals enough for burnt offerings. Before him all the nations are as nothing; they are regarded by him as worthless and less than nothing.

When Isaiah likens the nations to 'a drop in a bucket', he is probably referring to the drips that fall from the outside of a bucket when it is drawn from a well. They are a trifle, an irrelevance. So too are the nations when set beside God's great purposes.

He also says they are like the 'dust on the scales'. We do not worry if there is dust on the scales when we weigh something, because dust weighs nothing. Isaiah is saying that the nations come and go. The Egyptian Empire has come and gone. The eighth-century Assyrian Empire has come and gone. The sixth-century Babylonian Empire has come and gone. The Roman Empire has come and gone. The British Empire has come and gone. The Soviet Empire has come and gone. And today even the United States and China are like a drop in a bucket, compared to Almighty God. 'Behold your God.'

Look at the idols (vv. 18–20)

To whom, then, will you compare God? What image will you compare him to? As for an idol, a craftsman casts it, and a goldsmith overlays it with gold and fashions silver chains for it. A man too poor to present such an offering selects wood that will not rot. He looks for a skilled craftsman to set up an idol that will not topple.

Almost half of Isaiah 40–55 (including most of chapters

41, and 44–48) is about rival gods. Isaiah asks, 'To whom . . . will you compare God?' He ridicules an idol as a chunk of wood with silver and gold attached to it.

From verse 16 of chapter 44 he expands on this, describing a man making an idol from a block of wood. With half the wood he makes a fire with which to warm himself and bake bread. With the rest he makes a god and bows down to it and worships it, saying, 'Save me; you are my god' (Is 44:17). He has substituted something dead for the living God. As the apostle Paul put it, 'They exchanged the truth of God for a lie, and worshipped and served created things rather than the Creator' (Rom 1:25).

Isaiah has established the fact that God is the creator of all things, and there is nothing wrong with what he has made. Indeed, God himself 'saw all that he had made, and it was very good' (Gen 1:31). But we are not to worship created things and it is this kind of worship that Isaiah ridicules. Much of contemporary society takes good things and worships them. In the New Age movement we find the worship of Gaia, named after the earth-goddess of ancient Graeco-Roman myths: the earth is seen as a 'goddess' or 'mother', and some worship her as a living being. Others in our society devote themselves to the worship of money, the god Mammon (the Hebrew word for 'wealth' or 'money'). Others make sex their god and worship Aphrodite, the Greek goddess of beauty and erotic love. For still others, science and technology has become a god.

To all idol worshippers, Isaiah says in effect, 'Don't worship gods that will topple over. Worship the one true God who will not topple.' He is the one who created all things and nothing can compare with him. 'Behold your God.'

Look at history's great leaders (vv. 21–24)

Do you not know? Have you not heard? Has it not been told you from the beginning? Have you not understood since the earth was founded? He sits enthroned above the circle of the earth, and its people are like grasshoppers. He stretches out the heavens like a canopy, and spreads them out like a tent to live in. He brings princes to naught and reduces the rulers of this world to nothing. No sooner are they planted, no sooner are they sown, no sooner do they take root in the ground, than he blows on them and they wither, and a whirlwind sweeps them away like chaff.

God reduces the leaders and the rulers of the world to nothing. Where is Sennacherib? Where is Nebuchadnezzar? Or Cyrus, Alexander the Great, Napoleon, Hitler, or Mao? In the future, people will ask the same question of the world leaders, presidents and prime ministers of today, whether evil or good. God blows them away, just as in the desert a green plant can die and wither away in a day. No human being can compare to God. 'Behold your God.'

Look at the stars (vv. 25–26)

'To whom will you compare me? Or who is my equal?' says the Holy One. Lift your eyes and look to the heavens: Who created all these? He who brings out the starry host one by one, and calls them each by name. Because of his great power and mighty strength, not one of them is missing.

A universally awesome experience is to look at the stars. The poet Lord Byron called them 'the poetry of Heaven'. Human beings have been continually amazed and fascinated by them. The stars are also the subject of much science and exploration, as well as inspiring poetry and romance. Our star (the sun) is one of 100,000 million stars in our galaxy (the Milky Way). Our galaxy is one of over 100,000 million galaxies. The Babylonians worshipped the stars, but God created them. 'Behold your God.'

Look: he is a power-sharing God (vv. 27–31)

Why do you say, O Jacob, and complain, O Israel, 'My way is hidden from the Lord; my cause is disregarded by my God'? Do you not know? Have you not heard? The Lord is the everlasting God, the Creator of the ends of the earth. He will not grow tired or weary, and his understanding no-one can fathom. He gives strength to the weary and increases the power of the weak. Even youths grow tired and weary, and young men stumble and fall; but those who hope in the Lord will renew their strength. They will soar on wings like eagles; they will run and not grow weary, they will walk and not be faint.

Isaiah now moves to focus on what God wants to do in his world and with his people. The last part of chapter 40 says to us, 'Look, he is a power-sharing God,' as Tom Wright put it.

The Israelites, exhausted by their years in exile, were full of fear and felt abandoned. Their mood was that of many Christians today: despondent, cowed and despairing. They felt that God did not even know about their dark experience, still less that he cared enough to help them.

Isaiah asked two questions. First: Have we got a right vision of God? In verse 28 he summarises what he has said so far: 'The Lord is the everlasting God, the Creator of the ends of the earth.' He does not get tired and he is full of wisdom.

He then goes on to ask a second vital question: Have we got a right vision of what God wants to do with our lives? He is a power-sharing God. He gives strength to those who are weary and weighed down by life's pressures. He gives power to the weak, to those who lack inner strength. All of us get tired and weary—even youths. All of us stumble and fall—even energetic young people. But to those who 'hope in the Lord', that is, the people of God who are walking in a relationship with him, he makes this astonishing promise. God will share his power with them and will renew their strength. In verse 31, the promise comes in three parts.

First, 'they will soar on wings like eagles'. I once heard the American church leader Everett Fullam preach on the subject of eagles. He said:

Eagles do not fly—if you mean by that the flapping of wings to propel them from one place to another. Other birds do that, but not eagles. They have an inborn ability to discern wind currents. They do not go anywhere until the right breeze comes along. When it comes, they just let go, borne aloft by the wind. They do not have to flap their wings (how uncouth!)—eagles have the ability to lock their wings in place. All they do is to ride the wind. Other birds are afraid of storms. Eagles love a storm. It forces them higher and higher and higher.

Many Christians do their work for the Lord by the sweat of their brow. They join the cult of the white knuckles. They really 'work for God', like turkeys. Have you ever seen a turkey fly? They beat themselves into insensibility, propelling themselves across a farmyard.

They cannot get more than three feet off the ground. Eagle Christians do not serve by the grit of their teeth or sweat of their brow. It is service by the power of God through the wind of the Holy Spirit—discerning his purpose and then going with it, not trying to get him to bless your mess.[21]

This does not mean that we should not work hard, but that unless we do God's work in his strength, we shall get nowhere.

Secondly, 'they will run and not grow weary, they will walk and not be faint' (v. 31). They will run with urgency. There has been a growing sense among many Christians recently that it is time to act. We must respond to the urgent need to get the message of the gospel out to the world. God empowers us not just for quick sprints but to run the race with perseverance.

Thirdly, he enables us to walk with patience in spite of opposition. Those who hope in the Lord do not give up, but are given power to persevere.

So, we see that revival is a sovereign work of God, stemming from his greatness and power. Duncan Campbell writes: 'While recognising man's responsibility as the human agent, attention has been called again and again to the utter futility of human effort apart from the mighty manifestation of divine power.'[22] Our confidence that revival is coming is based on God's promise: his word and his character. He has revealed himself as a God who revives his people. He alone can bring about a true revival. And that is what he has promised to do. Nevertheless, it does not take place independently of human beings. We have a part to play. In the chapters that follow, we shall see some of the ways in which we are called to respond.

3

Whom Will God Use?

Isaiah 49:1–7

All true followers of Jesus Christ long for God to use them. If revival is coming we long to be part of it. How can we be involved? How can we be his servants?

The Chancellor of the Exchequer of Ethiopia (now Northern Sudan) was on his way home from Jerusa-

"Chancellor, what's the change in camel prices?"

lem. He was travelling in the ancient equivalent of a chauffeur-driven Rolls Royce. In Jerusalem he had bought, at great cost, a copy of a scroll of Isaiah. The evangelist Philip ran alongside saying, 'Do you understand what you are reading?' The Chancellor replied, 'How can I, unless someone explains it to me?' and he invited Philip to join him. He was studying one of the passages in Isaiah about the 'servant' (Is 53:7–8). He asked, 'Tell me, please, who is the prophet talking about, himself or someone else?' Then Philip began with that very passage and told him the good news about Jesus. The Chancellor of the Exchequer was converted and baptised, and the church in Africa began (see Acts 8:26 onwards). The question the Sudanese asked was a good one and much ink has since been spilled discussing it.

The title 'servant of the Lord' is one of great dignity reserved for individuals in a close relationship with God, such as Abraham, Moses and David (eg Genesis 26:24; Exodus 14:31; 2 Samuel 7:5). But in the four 'servant songs' (Is 42:1–4; 49:1–7; 50:4–9; 52:13—53:12) a distinctive concept of servanthood comes into sharper focus.

In some passages, the servant clearly refers to Israel (eg Isaiah 42:19; 48:20; 49:3). Many Jewish scholars still take the view that the servant is simply the people of Israel. However, in some of the passages the servant appears to be an individual (eg 49:1–2, 5). Moreover, the servant has a ministry and a mission to Israel (v. 5b). Who can this servant be? In 1921 the Old Testament scholar Mowinckel suggested it was the prophet himself. In 1931 he abandoned the idea because he realised that it involved the extremely hazardous assumption that he described his own death (52:10—53:12). Others have suggested that it is the prophet Jeremiah. Still others have suggested that it is Cyrus, king of Persia, although he is never called the servant. Many names have been suggested but none fits exactly.

The answer is probably more complex. The concept of the 'servant' can be understood in terms of a St Andrew's cross.

Originally God intended that all humankind should be his servant. After the Fall, God chose the whole nation of Israel to serve him (the widest part of the cross, on the left). But even his chosen race was not faithful to him. So the focus continued to narrow, until it became a mere 'faithful remnant'. Ultimately only one individual was completely faithful (the central, most narrow part of the cross). This was Jesus. Jesus revealed what Israel should have been. He was an Israelite sent to Israel. He was totally identified with his nation yet distinct from it. No king or prophet meets the description used in all the servant passages. Jesus does so—perfectly.

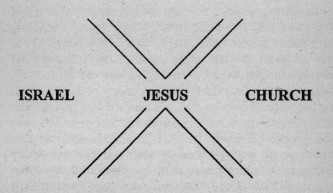

ISRAEL   JESUS   CHURCH

Where Israel failed, Jesus succeeded. Equally, it is God's plan that the church, through the victory of Christ and the power of the Holy Spirit, can and should succeed. So the St Andrew's cross broadens out again as the members of the church of Jesus Christ become the servants of God.

The servant passages, therefore, apply at three levels. At one level they applied to Israel or to a remnant in Israel. At this level Israel failed. At another level they apply to Jesus, the perfect Servant of God. Here the prophecies are fulfilled completely. But the servant passages also apply to the church and to our calling now to be the servants of God. The apostles frequently referred to themselves and the church as servants of God or servants of Christ (eg Acts 4:29; Romans 1:1; 1 Corinthians 4:1; Philippians 1:1). We need to read these passages in Isaiah at all three levels to recognise our part in them and to consider our response.

Isaiah's prophecy resonates through history, moving fluidly between past, present and future. Sometimes he looks at Israel, sometimes at Jesus and sometimes at his people, the church, throughout history. Once we understand this, we can better appreciate and, indeed, enter into the role of the Servant of the Lord.

What is the servant called to do? In Isaiah 49:1–6, the prophet outlines three main tasks of massive importance for the whole world. These are the identifying marks of God's servants.

Those who speak out (vv. 1–2)

Listen to me, you islands; hear this, you distant nations: Before I was born the Lord called me; from my birth he has made mention of my name. He made my mouth like a sharpened sword, in the shadow of his hand he hid me; he made me into a polished arrow and concealed me in his quiver.

First, the servant is called to declare God's word. The prophet summons the whole world, 'the islands' and the 'distant nations', to listen to him (49:1a). His call to do this even predates his birth: 'Before I was born the Lord called me; from my birth he has made mention of my name' (49:1b).

This was also true of Jeremiah. God said to him, 'Before I formed you in the womb I knew you, before you were born I set you apart; I appointed you as a prophet to the nations' (Jer 1:5). The same, of course, was true of Jesus, who was conceived by the power of the Holy Spirit. Before his birth his father Joseph was told, 'You are to give him the name Jesus, because he will save his people from their sins' (Mt 1:21). It was also true of the apostle Paul who wrote that God 'set me apart from my mother's womb' (Gal 1:15).

Not only is the servant called, but he is also equipped for the task. In the first servant song God says, 'Here is my servant, whom I uphold, my chosen one in whom I delight; I will put my Spirit on him . . .' (Is 42:1). He is equipped to speak out. 'He made my mouth like a sharpened sword' (49:2). In the third servant song, the servant says, 'The Sovereign Lord has given me an instructed tongue, to know the word that sustains the weary' (50:4a).

Paul has the same thought when he describes 'the sword of the Spirit' as the 'word of God' (Eph 6:17). Likewise, the writer of Hebrews says that 'the word of God is living and active. Sharper than any double-edged sword, it penetrates even to dividing soul and spirit, joints and marrow; it judges the thoughts and attitudes of the heart' (Heb 4:12). Supremely, the words of Jesus produced this effect (see, for example, Luke 7:36–50 and John 8:2–11).

In the book of Revelation the apostle John describes a vision of Jesus in which he sees coming 'out of his mouth . . . a sharp double-edged sword' (Rev 1:16). We, the church, have been equipped with the good news which goes to the heart of the human problem. When Peter preached the gospel on the day of Pentecost the people were 'cut to the heart' (Acts 2:37).

The prophet moves from the image of the sword to that of the arrow. 'He made me into a polished arrow' (49:2b). A good arrow is swift and goes straight to the target. It is devastatingly effective. But it takes time, skill and attention to detail to shape a proper arrow. First, it is roughly cut from a block of wood. Then it is filed. Then it is sandpapered. Finally it is polished. For us, also, there is a process of refining in our lives whereby God shapes us and purifies us that we might serve him better. Any imperfection in an arrow will prevent it from flying as the archer intended.

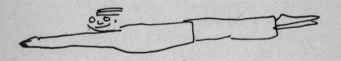

Moreover, the sword and the arrow might not be used immediately: 'in the shadow of his hand he hid me . . . and concealed me in his quiver'(v. 2). The servants of God often go through 'hidden years', a period of preparation. Joseph, in the book of Genesis, had a vision of what God wanted to do with his life at the age of seventeen. Thirteen years of slavery, suffering and imprisonment followed before eventually he was made Prime Minister of Egypt at the age of thirty. He was the man God used to save the whole nation of Israel. Jesus himself went through a period of thirty hidden years in Nazareth as well as forty days alone in the desert before he entered his public ministry. The apostle Paul, after his dramatic conversion, seems to have spent fourteen years of preparation before he began his effective public ministry (Gal 2:1). These examples should encourage us if we feel frustrated

'Hello, I'd like to talk to the Archbishop about my future.'

or under-used by God. Such times of waiting are not times to waste, but to use to increase our understanding of God and our intimacy with him. Indeed, God may spend many years preparing us and training us for a particular moment he has in mind.

'Hidden' years are not wasted years. The time Jesus spent working as a carpenter was not wasted. He was doing the will of his Father. In the same way our calling is to be the people of God; acting, thinking and sounding like him. Those who are called by God to do a job in the secular world, whether in paid employment or some other occupation, such as a mother bringing up children, should not feel that what they are doing is unimportant or insignificant. Work is good in itself (Gen 2:15). For most Christians it will be the main way in which they serve Christ, bringing benefit to the community and glorifying God.

God gave his servant Israel the task of declaring his word to the nations. Israel failed. Jesus, the perfect Servant, fulfilled it completely. Now we, the church, are his servants called to join him in the same task. We are called, equipped and prepared by God to speak out to this generation the good news of the gospel.

Those who live it out (v. 3)

He said to me, 'You are my servant, Israel, in whom I will display my splendour.'

The servant is called to demonstrate to other people what God is like: 'He said to me, "You are my servant, Israel, in whom I will display my splendour"' (v. 3). The expression 'display my splendour' occurs thirteen times in the Old Testament, nine of which are in Isaiah. Elsewhere the Lord 'shows his beauty' by what he does for the people (44:23; 60:21), but here it is by what they do for him. Here the servant (singular) is specifically called Israel. God had intended to display his splendour through the nation. However, Israel had not lived up to this intention and had not shown God's glory to the world.

Israel failed. Only Jesus, in his life, death and resurrection, has perfectly reflected the glory of God. John said of Jesus, 'We have seen his glory' (Jn 1:14). We are moving towards this: 'We, who with unveiled faces all reflect the Lord's glory, are being transformed into his likeness with ever-increasing glory, which comes from the Lord, who is the Spirit' (2 Cor 3:18).

US President Abraham Lincoln was discussing a certain senior official who had applied for a post in his government. He said to his advisors, 'We won't have him—I don't like his face.' His advisors retorted, 'He is not responsible for his face.' To which Lincoln replied, 'Oh yes he is—everyone over forty is responsible for his face!'

" Hymn number 52 "

God's glory or splendour is the outward shining of his inward character. Our faces fulfil the same function. They reflect what is going on inside. We need not work directly on our faces but we can allow God to work on our characters. We are called to be conformed to the likeness of Jesus Christ (Rom 8:29). As we 'keep in step with the Spirit', being obedient to whatever God may ask us to do, then the fruit of God's Spirit grows in our lives (see Galatians 5:22–25) and God's splendour shines out from our inward characters.

Malcolm Muggeridge described his first meeting with Mother Teresa like this:

> When I first set eyes on her, which is now some fifteen years ago—the occasion a casual TV interview—I at once realised that I was in the presence of someone of unique quality. This was not due to her appearance, which is homely, and unassuming, so that words like 'charm' or 'charisma' do not apply. Nor to her shrewdness and quick understanding, though these are very marked; nor even to her manifest piety and true humility and ready laughter. There is a phrase in one of the psalms that always, for me, evokes her presence: 'the beauty of holiness'—that special beauty, amounting to a kind of pervasive luminosity generated by a life dedicated wholly to loving God and His creation.[23]

Indira Gandhi (1917–84), Prime Minister of India from 1966–77 and 1980–84, wrote of Mother Teresa: 'To meet her is to feel utterly humble, to sense the power of tenderness, the strength of love . . . Gentleness, love, compassion radiate from her tiny person.'

Mother Teresa worked in the squalor of the Calcutta slums for forty-eight years. She was the first in her community to rise each day—unless the nuns hid her alarm clock. She said, 'I want to be the first to wake and see Jesus . . . I am doing my work with Jesus. I am doing it for Jesus . . . And therefore the results are His, not mine.' She died in Calcutta on 5 September 1997 at the age of eighty-seven. She had no fear of dying, for death, she said, 'is going home'.

Mary Kenny concluded her orbituary in *The Independent* on 6 September 1997 with these words: 'She changed the world that she was born into: she made an imaginative, inspirational and in many respects practical difference to millions of people's lives: and she did indeed accomplish something beautiful for God.'

It is not only as individuals but also as a Christian community that we are called to 'display' his 'splendour'. As we live the Christian life together, people will come into the church and recognise that God lives in and among us.

Those who go out (vv. 4–7)

But I said, 'I have laboured to no purpose; I have spent my strength in vain and for nothing. Yet what is due to me is in the Lord's hand, and my reward is with my God.' And now the Lord says—he who formed me in the womb to be his servant to bring Jacob back to him and gather Israel to himself, for I am honoured in the eyes of the Lord and my God has been my strength—he says: 'It is too small a thing for you to be my servant to restore the tribes of Jacob and bring back those of Israel I have kept. I will also make you a light for the Gentiles, that you may bring my salvation to the ends of the earth.' This is what the Lord says—the Redeemer and Holy One of Israel—to him who was despised and abhorred by the nation, to the servant of rulers: 'Kings will see you and rise up, princes will see

*and bow down, because of the Lord, who is faithful, the
Holy One of Israel, who has chosen you.'*

Thirdly, the servant is called to be a blessing to the
world. He has a glorious and high calling: to 'bring
justice to the nations' (Is 42:1) and, ultimately, to bring
God's 'salvation to the ends of the earth' (49:6). With
such an important task to complete, it could be easy
to become discouraged. This happens particularly
when God's servants rely on their own strength and
not on his. 'But I said, "I have laboured to no purpose;
I have spent my strength in vain and for nothing. Yet
what is due to me is in the Lord's hand, and my
reward is with my God"' (v. 4).

This again is the pattern in Scripture for God's
servants. First, the promise, then the difficulties and
finally the fulfilment. For example, Abraham was promised a child, but as time went by nothing happened.
Only years later was the promise fulfilled. Moses was
called to take God's people out of Egypt and into the
promised land. But everything went badly wrong
before the promise was fulfilled: at first, Pharaoh would
not let them leave Egypt, and then there followed forty
years of wandering in the desert. Jesus himself must
have experienced discouragement when so many
deserted him and fell away. He could justifiably have
felt frustration, hopelessness and despair. A time of
testing is an opportunity for God to develop our faith.
During these times we need to say, 'Yet what is due to
me is in the Lord's hand, and my reward is with my
God' (v. 4b). God rewards faithfulness and not results.

Often we have to go through a time of testing because
God's vision is far bigger than ours. The servant has
spoken. Now God speaks to the servant. The calling is
not simply 'to bring Jacob back to him and gather Israel

to himself'. God says, 'I am calling you to something immeasurably greater than you ever imagined.' He is calling the servant not merely to bring God's people back to him, but to be a 'light to the Gentiles' and to bring his salvation to the ends of the earth.

This was God's original calling to the people of Israel. They were intended to be an example to the whole world. Again they failed. Only in Jesus, the perfect Israelite, was the prophecy fulfilled. When Simeon took the baby Jesus in his arms he recognised that he was the one who was to be 'a light . . . to the Gentiles' (Lk 2:32). The apostle Paul used this verse time and again when the Jews were angry because the ordinary people in Asia Minor were responding enthusiastically to his message (eg Acts 13:47).

Jesus commissioned his disciples 'to go and make disciples of all nations' (Mt 28:18–19). Now we, the church, must never lose sight of this worldwide vision. We are called to be 'a light for the Gentiles' and to take God's salvation 'to the ends of the earth' (49:6).

There is still a long way to go. The whole Bible has been translated into around 350 languages. Just over 2,000 have at least one book of the Bible but over 4,000 languages still do not have even one book translated. This group represents over 350 million people. There are still many people who have never heard the gospel. We must never lose sight of our calling to take God's light and his salvation to the ends of the earth. Today, with modern technology, this could be achieved.

The good news is that never before in history has such a high percentage of the world's population been exposed to the gospel. It is estimated that 170 million Christians are committed to praying every day for revival. Already the church is growing faster than ever before and Christianity is gaining more adherents than any other religion. Indeed, it is growing at three times the rate of the population explosion. More Muslims in Iran have come to know Christ over the past ten years than during the previous thousand years. In Africa, 20,000 people a day are becoming Christians. Some estimate that there may now be as many as 100 million Christians in China alone.

"...plus our home group obviously"

However, all this amazing potential has come about at a cost. The prophet now zooms in on one individual servant. In a foreshadowing of Isaiah 53 he speaks of 'him who was despised and abhorred by the nation' (v. 7). In each servant song this element of suffering increases. In the third servant song (Is 50:6) the servant suffers a judicial act of flogging, gratuitous torture and personal humiliation. Jesus knew what it was to be the suffering servant of God. He said, 'For even the Son of Man did not come to be served, but to serve, and to give his life as a ransom for many' (Mk 10:45).

The one who 'humbled himself . . . God exalted'
(Phil 2:8–9). The servant glorifies God (v. 3). Now
God glorifies the servant (v. 7). The prophet says of
the servant, 'Kings will see you and rise up, princes
will see and bow down, because of the Lord, who is
faithful, the Holy One of Israel, who has chosen you'
(v. 7). This was fulfilled when the Magi came to worship Jesus (Mt 2:1–12). It was fulfilled in the fourth
century when Constantine became the first Roman
Emperor to bow the knee to Jesus. It was fulfilled in
988 when Vladimir became the first Russian prince to
embrace the Christian faith. It has been fulfilled in the
last 200 years as African kings and princes have
bowed the knee to the King of kings. Maybe in the
next hundred years we will see the Emperor of Japan
or the King of Saudi Arabia worshipping Jesus.
Whether we do or not, one day every knee will
bow. In the future, Pilate, Herod, Annas, Caiaphas,
Alexander the Great, Napoleon, Hitler, Saddam Hus-
sein and every other ruler will bow the knee to Jesus.
Some will do so voluntarily and some under compul-
sion. On that day those who are his servants now will
reign with him for ever.

Our task as God's servants today is to tell others
now so that they will rejoice and reign with him,
rather than face his terrifying judgement against
them. We need to tell people the good news and
warn them of the dangers of rejecting God. God has
called us and equipped us. His splendour is on us, so
we are not to be discouraged. He is calling us to an
immeasurably greater vision than we ever imagined
possible. That which Israel failed to do, that which
Jesus did supremely, is now the task of the church: to
be 'a light for the Gentiles', that we 'may bring . . .
salvation to the ends of the earth'. The gospel is public

truth for the whole world. We need to pray and work towards a revival which is not just local or even national, but one which extends 'to the ends of the earth'.

God has promised to bring revival. Every revival is a sovereign work of God. Nevertheless he has chosen to use his servants to bring about his purposes. We, the church, are his servants today. The church and those who are members of it need to respond to his call and be willing to go through the process of being equipped and prepared to speak out the good news. Yet words are not enough. Our character and our life must reflect our words. Our lifestyle must be consistent with our message. Further, if we want God to use us, we must be willing to go out and 'bring' his salvation to the ends of the earth.

All of us who are members of the church have the potential to be used by God in revival. In his essay *The Twelve Men*, which comments on the British jury system, G. K. Chesterton wrote, 'Whenever our civilization wants a library to be catalogued, or a solar system discovered, or any other trifle of this kind, it uses up its specialists. But when it wishes anything done which is really serious, it collects twelve of the ordinary men standing around. The same thing was done, if I remember right, by the Founder of Christianity.'

4

What Is at the Heart of Revival?

Isaiah 49:8—50:3

This is what the Lord says: 'In the time of my favour I will answer you, and in the day of salvation I will help you; I will keep you and will make you to be a covenant for the people, to restore the land and to reassign its desolate inheritances, to say to the captives, "Come out," and to those in darkness, "Be free!"'

Alex and Peggy Buchanan have considerable personal handicaps. Peggy has multiple sclerosis and is confined to a wheelchair. Alex has had a stroke and is paralysed on one side of his face. They have endured much suffering, yet they never complain. Rather, they spend their time listening to the complaints of others who seek their wise and often prophetic counsel.

When speaking to Christian leaders Alex Buchanan often says, 'God loves you unconditionally, wholeheartedly and continually.' He gets them to repeat it over and over again, saying it to one another until they finally get the point. He also adds, 'God approves of you.' On one occasion he took me aside and asked, 'Do you believe God approves of you?' I found it an extremely difficult question to answer, and said, 'I am so conscious of my own weaknesses.'

Alex replied, 'We all are. God wants you to know that he loves you and approves of you.'

The Old Testament covenant came into being through God's unconditional, wholehearted and continual love for his people. The Hebrew word *hesed* describes this kind of love, often translated as 'loving-kindness' or 'grace'. In effect God said, 'You have become the people of Yahweh, therefore be the people of Yahweh' ('Yahweh' is a Hebrew name for God). He chose them even though they did not deserve it. He demonstrated his free and unconditional love. 'The Lord did not set his affection on you and choose you because you were more numerous than other peoples, for you were the fewest of all peoples. But it was because the Lord loved you . . . ' (Deut 7:7–8).

The Law was God's gift and the keeping of the Law was an expression of faith and obedience. However, God's people failed to keep it and their disloyalty and rebellion had disastrous results, culminating in the fall of Jerusalem in 587 BC. The prophets indicated that God had every right to terminate the covenant, but although he had good reasons for doing so, instead of destruction he promised restoration, renewal and revival. He said: 'In the time of my favour I will answer you, and in the day of salvation I will help you; I will keep you and will make you to be a covenant for the people, to restore the land and to reassign its desolate inheritances, to say to the captives, "Come out," and to those in darkness, "Be free!"' (Is 49:8–9a).

The passage that follows expresses God's love for his people. It is all about God's 'compassion' (vv. 10, 13, 15). The word 'compassion' means 'love that is emotionally moved'.[24] So certain is the promise of restoration that the prophet composes a hymn about the love of God. Other gods made the people suffer out of malice. But the people of God had not suffered in exile because of God's malice. God is a God of love and compassion who demonstrates that love for his people. In this passage we see five visual aids (pictures or analogies) of the love of God. They are interspersed with three objections which are raised against the suggestion that God could be about to bring restoration and revival.

The first analogy of love: the shepherd (vv. 9–13)

'They will feed beside the roads and find pasture on every barren hill. They will neither hunger nor thirst, nor will the desert heat or the sun beat upon them. He who has compassion on them will guide them and lead them beside springs of water. I will turn all my mountains into roads, and my highways will be raised up. See, they will come from afar—some from the north, some from the west, some from the region of Aswan.' Shout for joy, O heavens; rejoice, O earth; burst into song, O mountains! For the Lord comforts his people and will have compassion on his afflicted ones.

The relationship between sheep and their shepherd is quite different in Palestine from elsewhere. For example, in Britain sheep are usually kept for killing and eating, but in Palestine they are valuable for their wool. Hence sheep often stay with the same shepherd for many years and each has its own individual name. The word 'pastor' is the Latin word for a shepherd, and in the same way God loves, cares for and provides for his people.

"Eric, Janet, over here please"

First, this is a picture of provision. 'They will feed beside the roads and find pasture on every barren hill. They will neither hunger nor thirst, nor will the desert heat or the sun beat upon them' (vv. 9b–10a). The shepherd will ensure that 'pasturage will be ready at hand, meeting them at every step and even the barren hill will be there to meet their need'.[25] If we could really grasp this it would save us a lot of unnecessary anxiety.

Secondly, the shepherd protects his sheep. The Palestinian shepherd carried a staff, a short wooden club which had a lump of wood at the end often studded with nails. It usually had a slit in the handle at the top, through which a thong passed, which could be looped over the shepherd's belt. A staff was the weapon with which he defended himself and his flock against marauding beasts and robbers. Dr W. M. Thompson in *The Land and the Book* describes 'desperate fights with savage beasts . . . thieves and robbers . . . the faithful shepherd putting his life in his hands to defend his flock. Sometimes he had to lay it down in the contest. For example, one faithful shepherd fought three Bedouin robbers until he was hacked to pieces with their khanjars. . . . He died among the sheep he was defending.'[26] Again, if we could grasp this it would save us from many of our fears.

Thirdly, the shepherd guides the sheep (v. 10b). In Palestine the shepherd walked in front of the sheep to see if the path was safe, and sometimes the sheep had to be encouraged to follow. One traveller recalled that he saw a shepherd leading his flock across a stream. The sheep were unwilling to cross, but the shepherd finally solved the problem by carrying one of the lambs across. When the mother saw her lamb on the other side, she crossed too and the rest followed her. The shepherd carried a rod to catch and pull back any straying sheep. He also had a sling, used partly in self-defence and partly because there were no sheep dogs in Palestine. When a shepherd wished to call back a sheep which was straying from the flock, he would fit a stone into his sling and land it just in front of the straying sheep's nose as a warning to turn back.

God, as the shepherd of Israel, will lead his people back out of exile. In his love, he will make even obstacles serve his purpose. 'I will turn all my mountains into roads and my highways will be raised up' (v. 11). The mountains are his and he can do with them as he likes.

This is the same thought that Paul had when he wrote, 'And we know that in all things God works for the good of those who love him, who have been called according to his purpose' (Rom 8:28). Even when life seems to put up barriers against us we might discover that they are in fact part of God's plan for us. Both good and bad experiences can be the raw material through which God works out his purposes in our lives.

Jesus picks up the picture of the good shepherd and applies it to himself:

> He calls his own sheep by name and leads them out . . . . He goes on ahead of them, and his sheep follow him because they know his voice . . . I am the good shepherd. The good shepherd lays down his life for the sheep . . . I know my sheep and my sheep know me—just as the Father knows me and I know the Father—and I lay down my life for the sheep (Jn 10:3–15).

The second analogy of love: the parent (vv. 14–15)

But Zion said, 'The Lord has forsaken me, the Lord has forgotten me.' 'Can a mother forget the baby at her breast and have no compassion on the child she has borne? Though she may forget, I will not forget you!'

Immediately the objection is raised that God would not restore his people: 'But Zion said, "The Lord has forsaken me, the Lord has forgotten me"' (v. 14). The people felt forsaken and forgotten, as if God did not care about them. The prophet replies: 'Can a mother forget the baby at her breast and have no compassion on the child she has borne? Though she may forget, I will not forget you!' (v. 15).

It is possible for a parent to forget a child. My parents-in-law told me of such an incident. They had a friend who had married late in life and had a son. On one occasion he and his wife went out to dinner with my parents-in-law. They brought their baby and put him in an upstairs room. As they were leaving, my father-in-law asked, 'Haven't you forgotten something?' The man replied, 'What's that, old boy? Did I leave my hat?' He had totally forgotten about his son.

It is much harder for a mother to forget 'the baby at her breast', yet even that is possible. But it is impossible for God to forget his people: his love is even greater than a mother's for her baby. The Bible uses both male and female imagery to help us understand the nature of God. God's love for us is like that of a perfect mother and a perfect father. One of the ways in which Paul describes the Holy Spirit is as the 'Spirit of sonship' (Rom 8:15).

Many today lack real experience of parental love. I recently came across an example of this from *Sports Illustrated* magazine. Greg Norman, for many years the best golfer in the world, intimidates most other professional golfers with his cool temperament. He learned his hard-nosed tactics from his father. 'I used to see my father, getting off a plane or something, and I'd want to hug him,' he recalled once. 'But he'd only shake my hand.' Commenting on his aloofness going into the 1996 US Masters tournament, Norman said, 'Nobody really knows me out here.'

After leading from the start, Norman blew a six-shot lead in the last round, losing to Nick Faldo.

The journalist wrote: 'As Faldo made one last thrust into Norman's heart with a 15-foot birdie putt on the 72nd [final] hole, the two of them came towards each other, Norman trying to smile, looking for a handshake and finding himself in the warmest embrace instead.

'As they held that hug, held it even as both of them cried, Norman changed just a little. "I wasn't crying because I'd lost," Norman said the next day. "I've lost a lot of golf tournaments before. I'll lose a lot more. I cried because I'd never felt that from another man before, I've never had a hug like that in my life."'[27]

'The Spirit himself testifies with our spirit that we are God's children' (Rom 8:16). As the Holy Spirit fills people, they often experience exactly this. One person wrote to me, 'I know now with assurance that God loves me as a father.' Another said, 'I had an incredible sense of God holding me and saying that he is my father: no man, organisation or church will ever be able to break that bond. . . . I have never been so close to God.' Another simply said, 'It was a new thing for me. . . . God showed his fatherhood and his love for me.'

The third analogy of love: the engraver (vv. 16–23)

'See, I have engraved you on the palms of my hands; your walls are ever before me. Your sons hasten back, and those who laid you waste depart from you. Lift up your eyes and look around; all your sons gather and come to you. As

surely as I live,' declares the Lord, 'you will wear them all as ornaments; you will put them on, like a bride.

'Though you were ruined and made desolate and your land laid waste, now you will be too small for your people, and those who devoured you will be far away. The children born during your bereavement will yet say in your hearing, "This place is too small for us; give us more space to live in." Then you will say in your heart, "Who bore me these? I was bereaved and barren; I was exiled and rejected. Who brought these up? I was left all alone, but these— where have they come from?"'

This is what the Sovereign Lord says: 'See, I will beckon to the Gentiles, I will lift up my banner to the peoples; they will bring your sons in their arms and carry your daughters on their shoulders. Kings will be your foster fathers, and their queens your nursing mothers. They will bow down before you with their faces to the ground; they will lick the dust at your feet. Then you will know that I am the Lord; those who hope in me will not be disappointed.'

The Babylonians, as many do today, used tattoos to remind them of the person they loved. A tattoo demonstrates commitment. A tattoo is extremely difficult (although not impossible) to remove and therefore expresses the confidence that a relationship will never go wrong. Unfortunately, human relationships do go wrong. Nevertheless God uses this picture in his commitment to us. 'See,' he says, 'I have engraved you on the palms of my hands' (v. 16a). It is difficult to read this without thinking of the cross, the hammer and the nails. Jesus' love and commitment to us was total, taking him to the depths of suffering, the cruel wounds evident for all to see. When Thomas saw Jesus' palms he cried out, 'My Lord and my God' (Jn 20:28).

The evidence for God's ongoing commitment to his people will be seen, says the prophet, in a dramatic and spectacular restoration. 'Your walls are ever before me' (v. 16b). He promises the rebuilding of Jerusalem and the repopulation of the land. People will say, 'Where on earth did all these people come from?' (vv. 19–21) and the place will seem too small (v. 20). Even kings and queens will come in on that day (v. 23). He looks forward to a triumphant return with vast numbers of people.

The fourth analogy of love: the conqueror (vv. 24–26)

Can plunder be taken from warriors, or captives rescued from the fierce? But this is what the Lord says: 'Yes,

*captives will be taken from warriors, and plunder retrieved
from the fierce; I will contend with those who contend with
you, and your children I will save. I will make your
oppressors eat their own flesh; they will be drunk on their
own blood, as with wine. Then all mankind will know that
I, the Lord, am your Saviour, your Redeemer, the Mighty
One of Jacob.'*

Another objection is raised. Even God is not strong
enough to bring about restoration: 'Can plunder be
taken from warriors, or captives rescued from the
fierce?' (v. 24). To this objection the prophet replies
that God's love is like a conqueror (vv. 25–26). He is
quite strong enough to carry out his purposes. He
assures those who object that God cannot do it,
'God can and God will.' God's love for his people is
immensely strong and determined.

God's covenant with his people followed a similar
pattern to many sovereignty treaties in the ancient
Middle East, such as the Hittite treaties of the second
millennium BC. The Hittites were a powerful people
who dominated much of Canaan at that time. The
Hittite king, as conqueror, entered into a relationship
with the people he conquered. The treaties began with
an introduction of the name and position of the over-
lord. This was followed by a historical prologue giving
the setting for the covenant relationship, rehearsing
the way in which the king conquered the people.
Then came the terms of the treaty, that there were to
be no other allies without permission, that dues were
to be paid, and that representatives were to appear
annually to reaffirm their loyalty. Title deeds of all
properties were to be put on deposit with the conquering administration and brought out to be read
from time to time. The legal procedure had to be

witnessed and there were added to the agreement sanctions and benefits, to come into effect dependent on the good behaviour (or otherwise) of the conquered nation.

God's covenant in Exodus 20 onwards follows a similar pattern. There is a title, prologue and stipulations (for example, God's people were to have no other gods). The covenant was to be deposited in the Ark and read regularly. There were witnesses and blessings and curses.

The one who is the 'conqueror' of Israel has the power to conquer other nations. He will fight on behalf of his people: 'I will contend with those who contend with you' (v. 25). Winston Churchill was a fervent patriot: he loved his country and his people. He was also unshakeable in his resistance to tyranny and his commitment to the defeat of Hitler. In a much greater way God is committed to his people and will fight against those who oppress them.

The fifth analogy of love: the husband (50: 1–3)

This is what the Lord says: 'Where is your mother's certificate of divorce with which I sent her away? Or to which of my creditors did I sell you? Because of your sins you were sold; because of your transgressions your mother was sent away. When I came, why was there no-one? When I called, why was there no-one to answer? Was my arm too short to ransom you? Do I lack the strength to rescue you? By a mere rebuke I dry up the sea, I turn rivers into a desert; their fish rot for lack of water and die of thirst. I clothe the sky with darkness and make sackcloth its covering.'

We have seen that the first objection was that God *would* not do it, and the second that he *could* not. The third objection raised against the promise of restoration and revival was that God *should* not do it. The people were saying God had divorced them because of their sins. They felt they had been sold to his creditors.

God replies through his prophet that although it was their weakness and their sin which caused the exile, God is able to restore them. He has not divorced them or sold them into slavery. He asks, 'Where is your mother's certificate of divorce with which I sent her away? Or to which of my creditors did I sell you?' (Is 50:1). No one is too far out of God's reach. He is married to his people.

In the Bible, God's love for his people is often likened to a husband's love for his wife. Isaiah states, 'For your Maker is your husband' (54:5). Through the prophets Ezekiel and Malachi God accuses his people of being an 'adulterous wife! You preferred strangers to your own husband!' (Ezek 16:32). Most famously, Paul speaks of marriage and a husband's love for his wife as an analogy of Christ's love for his church (Eph 5:22–33). Finally, the church is described in the book of Revelation as the 'bride of Christ'.

The heart of revival is God's love for his people. Every revival involves a fresh experience of the Holy Spirit who pours out God's love in our hearts (Rom 5:5) and his people love him in return. The word for 'pours' is the same word as is used in Acts 2:12, when Peter reminds the crowd that the Holy Spirit will be poured out on all flesh. As in Acts, the outpouring of God's love through the Holy Spirit leads to revival.

Howell Harris, who was so powerfully used in revival in Wales, described how, on 18 June 1735, he met with God. It was so real that he referred to it often throughout his life:

I felt suddenly my heart melting within me like wax before the fire with love to God my Saviour; and also felt not only love, peace, etc., but a longing to be dissolved, and to be with Christ. Then was a cry in my inmost soul which I was totally unacquainted with before. Abba Father! Abba Father! I could not help calling God my Father; I knew that I was His child, and that He loved me and heard me. My soul, being filled and satiated, crying, 'Tis enough, I am satisfied. Give me strength, and I will follow Thee through fire and water.' I could say I was happy indeed. There was in me a well of water, springing up to everlasting life, (John 4:14). The love of God was shed abroad in my heart by the Holy Ghost, (Romans 5:5).[28]

Sarah Edwards, who was involved with her husband Jonathan in the Great Awakening in New England, wrote of her experience in January 1742:

All night I continued in a constant, clear and lively sense of the heavenly sweetness of Christ's excellent and transcendent love, of his nearness to me and of my dearness to him . . . I seemed . . . to perceive a glow of divine love come down from the heart of Christ in heaven, into my heart, in a constant stream, like a stream or pencil of sweet light. At the same time, my heart and soul all flowed out in love to Christ; so that there seemed to be a constant flowing and reflowing of heavenly and divine love, from Christ's heart to mine; and I appeared to myself to float or swim, in these bright, sweet beams of the love of Christ . . . So far as I am capable of making a comparison, I think that what I felt each minute . . . was worth more than all the outward comfort and pleasure which I had enjoyed in my whole life put together. It was a pure delight, which fed and satisfied the soul.[29]

In 1762, the Holy Spirit was poured out in Wales in exceptional profusion. The hymnwriter, William Williams, described what happened:

For there fell upon us the sweet breath of the love of the Lord . . . The cloud melted away, the sun shone, we drank of the fruit of the vines of the promised land, and we were made to rejoice. Gone was unbelief, gone guilt, gone fear, gone a timid, cowardly spirit, lack of love, envy, suspicion, together with all the poisonous worms that tormented us before; and in their place came love, faith, hope, a joyful spirit, with a glorious multitude of the graces of the Holy Spirit.[30]

Professor Raniero Cantalamessa, formerly a member of the International Theological Commission, and now preacher to the Papal household, wrote:

The whole Bible, St Augustine observed, does nothing but tell of God's love (*Cat. rud.* 1, 8, 4; PL 40, 319); it is, so to say, full of it. This is the message that supports and explains all the other messages. The love of God is the answer to all the 'why's' in the Bible; the why of Creation, the why of the Incarnation, the why of Redemption . . . If the written word of the Bible could be changed into a spoken word and become one single voice, this voice, more powerful than the roaring of the sea would cry out: *The Father loves you!* (Jn 16:27). Everything that God does and says in the Bible is love—even God's anger is nothing but love. God 'is' love![31]

As we experience God's love for us we receive a new love for him. 'We love because he first loved us' (1 Jn 4:19). So we are enabled to fulfil the greatest commandment: 'Love the Lord your God with all your heart and with all your soul and with all your mind' (Mt 22:37) and the second to 'love your neighbour as yourself' (Mt 22:39). Love, according to Jonathan Edwards, is the 'most eminent' distinguishing mark of the Holy Spirit in revival. He writes: 'If the spirit that is at work among a people operates as a spirit of love to God and man, it is a sure sign that it is

the Spirit of God . . . It is love that arises from appre-
hension of the wonderful riches of the free grace and
sovereignty of God's love to us in Jesus Christ.'[32]

It is God's love and only his love that can bring
restoration and revival. At the heart of every revival is
God's heart of love for his people. The answer to the
objection that God will not bring about revival is that
he loves us and therefore he will. The answer to the
objection that he cannot do it is that his love is so
great that he can. The answer to the objection that he
should not is that he loves us so much that in spite of
our failings he shall. God loves us 'unconditionally,
wholeheartedly and continually'. At the heart of revival is the love of God.

5

What Is the Message of Revival?
Isaiah 52:13—53:12

When Helen Shapiro toured with the Beatles in early
1963, she was top of the bill and they were the sup-
porting act. By the time she was fifteen, two of her
records had reached number one in the UK pop
charts. The second, 'Walking Back to Happiness',
made her an international superstar. But after that
her personal life began to fall apart.

Having been brought up in a traditional Jewish
home in the heart of London's Jewish community,
she had a very strong sense of her Jewish identity.
However, her interests soon turned to spiritism, Buddhism, psychic phenomena and reincarnation. But
she envied the faith of her musical director who was
a Christian, so one night she cried out, 'OK, Jesus. You
say you are the Messiah. If you are, show me.'

She started to read the Old Testament and was
amazed to find the prophecy, 'For to us a child is
born, to us a son is given . . . ' (Is 9:6). Helen had
always thought that this verse was in the New Testament because she used to see it on Christmas cards.
She then read in Micah that the Messiah was to be
born in Bethlehem and in Isaiah that he would be
born of a virgin. She saw in Psalm 22 a graphic
account of the circumstances surrounding Jesus'

death on the cross. She then found Isaiah 53, which spoke of his great sacrifice.

She remembers thinking, 'Why don't I know this? Why didn't somebody tell me? Nobody has ever preached the gospel to me in a Jewish way.' So she read and reread the messianic prophecies and then moved on to the New Testament. Eventually, she prayed and asked Jesus to come into her life. Within a year, her mother and her boyfriend (now her husband) also came to know Christ. She now says, 'There are more Jewish people now coming to know the Messiah worldwide than at any time since the 1st century AD.'[33]

This chapter of the Old Testament is the one most often quoted in the New Testament. The scholar Joachim Jeremias wrote that, 'No other passage from the Old Testament was as important to the Church as Isaiah 53.'[34] The New Testament writers quote specific verses as having been fulfilled in Jesus, and Jesus himself often referred to this chapter. His followers did the same: in Acts 8 (as we have seen in Chapter 2) Philip interprets this passage to an Ethiopian treasury official by explaining that it refers to Jesus. Christians down the centuries have followed his example. This is the last and greatest of the four servant songs, in which Isaiah seems to focus on just one person: the person at the centre of the St Andrew's cross (see page 39).

According to the Koran, Jesus did not die on the cross. According to Nietzsche, the cross was a sign of weakness. The followers of Sun Myung Moon believe the cross was a mistake and a failure. This passage from Isaiah indicates that Jesus would die on a cross, and that this would be neither a mistake nor a failure. This was a death that was planned before the foundation of the world, and predicted hundreds of years beforehand.

The passage is a carefully scripted poem with five stanzas of three verses each. Each verse is one line longer than the one before, which creates a sense of mounting excitement. Stanzas one and five are the words of God about the servant. Stanzas two and four are the people looking on in astonishment. Stanza three (Is 53:4–6) is the pivot on which the whole poem turns. Indeed it is the pivot on which the whole of Isaiah turns. Indeed it is the central message of the whole Bible and of the whole of world history.

The first line of each stanza gives the theme, which is then expanded in the rest of the stanza. In each stanza we see an extraordinary contrast. We will look in turn at each of these five contrasts.

First contrast: apparent failure and actual success (52:13–15)

See, my servant will act wisely; he will be raised and lifted up and highly exalted. Just as there were many who were appalled at him—his appearance was so disfigured beyond that of any man and his form marred beyond human likeness—so will he sprinkle many nations, and kings will shut their mouths because of him. For what they were not told, they will see, and what they have not heard, they will understand.

The stanza starts with God singing about his servant, whom we now know to be his Son. It is about the servant who gets to the top, who starts with humiliation and ends with honour.

In 1876 Rufus Isaacs, a sixteen-year-old boy known as 'the Rake of Belsize' ran away from his father's fruit farm. He went to sea on a ship called *The Blair Athole*, and worked barefoot as a deckhand. He sailed round the world. When he left India the captain heard him say, 'I shall return, but not on the forecastle head.' When he got back to England he eventually settled down and at the age of twenty-three studied to become a lawyer.

With iron self-discipline and determination he rose in his career. He became Solicitor General, Attorney General (the first to sit in the Cabinet) and eventually Lord Chief Justice. He went as Ambassador to Washington, and also became President of ICI. He was the last Liberal Foreign Secretary and was leader of the House of Commons. He was Lord Warden of the Cinque Ports. He returned to India as Viceroy between 1921 and 1926. He was made a Baron in 1914, Viscount in 1916, Earl in 1917 and Marquess of Reading in 1926. Rufus Isaacs was the first man to go from commoner to Marquess since Wellington. Unlike the servant, his ascent was not through suffering and rejection. But like the servant he started at the bottom and ended at the top.

Although Jesus was always the Son of God, he was not always recognised as such by the people around. Indeed, in his letter to the Philippians, Paul writes that Jesus 'humbled himself' to become the servant of all. God says about his servant, 'He will be raised and lifted up and highly exalted' (v.13). The prophet seems to get a glimpse of the resurrection, ascension and exaltation of Jesus.

How was this exaltation achieved? Martin Luther said, 'The cross shatters human expectations.' Isaiah here foretells Jesus' scourging and death. The last image of Jesus on earth (apart from his resurrection appearances) is that of a man with his face bruised and ripped by thorns, his back in ribbons, his hands and feet pierced and his side scarred. The stanza begins with the servant being lifted up, moves to apparent failure and is finally elevated back to glory.

The sufferings of the servant will have an impact across the world: 'so will he sprinkle many nations' (v. 15). The Israelite practice of sprinkling the blood of sacrificed animals (eg Exodus 29:19–20; 2 Chronicles 29:22) was a rite of purification and cleansing from sin. In the same way, Jesus' death was a sacrifice made in order to purify us from sin, and indeed, to remove it from us for ever: 'The blood of goats and bulls . . . sprinkled on those who are ceremonially unclean sanctify them so that they are outwardly clean. How much more then, will the blood of Christ . . . cleanse our consciences . . . so that we may serve the living God!' (Heb 9:13–14).

In this first stanza, we see an extraordinary combination introduced—suffering and honour, sadness and joy. Such things do not normally go together in the world. Honour is sought, and suffering is regarded as unavoidable. They are seen as opposites, but here they are the two sides of the same coin. With God, apparent failure may actually be success. Those who humble themselves will be exalted.

Second contrast: our view and God's view (53:1–3)

Who has believed our message and to whom has the arm of the Lord been revealed? He grew up before him like a tender shoot, and like a root out of dry ground. He had no beauty or majesty to attract us to him, nothing in his appearance that we should desire him. He was despised and rejected by others, a man of sorrows, and familiar with suffering. Like one from whom people hide their faces he was despised, and we esteemed him not.

The people of Israel thought that there was no way they could miss God's Messiah. They knew that he would be a great political and kingly figure like Moses or David. When the people look on and observe his suffering they misunderstand. 'Who has believed our message and to whom has the arm of the Lord been revealed?' (v. 1). So often, even the people of God do not recognise 'the arm [meaning the power] of the Lord'. Even Peter could not believe that God's way would be through crucifixion (see Matthew 16:22; Mark 8:32).

In this stanza we see a contrast between man's view and God's view. God sees the servant as 'a tender shoot, and like a root out of dry ground' (v. 2). He is like a green shoot in a desert. Human beings did not see him like that. 'He had no beauty or majesty to attract us to him, nothing in his appearance that we should desire him' (v. 2b). There was nothing especially attractive in his human appearance to commend Jesus. He was not an impressive figure. He was a carpenter's son from a far-off provincial town. 'He was despised and rejected by men, a man of sorrows, and familiar with suffering. Like one from whom men hide their faces he was despised, and we esteemed him not' (v. 3). When Jesus was crucified, people looked away. They were ashamed and embarrassed and did not know how to cope.

Simon Weston, the Falklands veteran, was disfigured in a bomb attack on the *Sir Galahad*. He underwent reconstruction of his face through plastic surgery, but was still disfigured. In his book,[35] he recalls that he could not face people and nobody could face him. He describes how it feels to walk down the street and have people look away from you in horror. The prophet foresees that Jesus will be 'like one from whom men hide their faces. He was despised, and we esteemed him not.' Although he had come to save Israel, Israel rejected him.

In the film *City Lights*, Charlie Chaplin plays the tramp who loves a blind girl. He saves up and finally manages to pay for the blind girl to have an operation so that she can see, and her sight is restored. Later, she looks through a window, sees the tramp, and, not realising who he is, laughs at him. Jesus is still so often rejected by the people he came to save. Their view of him contrasts starkly with God's view.

Third contrast: our sin and his suffering (53:4–6)

Surely he took up our infirmities and carried our sorrows, yet we considered him stricken by God, smitten by him and afflicted. But he was pierced for our transgressions, he was crushed for our iniquities; the punishment that brought us peace was upon him, and by his wounds we are healed. We all, like sheep, have gone astray, each of us has turned to his own way; and the Lord has laid on him the iniquity of us all.

Why did the servant have to die? A normal understanding of suffering in biblical times was to think that the person must have been 'stricken by God' (v. 4b). It is true that there is a link in the Bible between sin and suffering. But it is not necessarily our sin that leads to our suffering (see, for example, the book of Job and John 9:1–2). Here, the servant is indeed suffering but not for his own sin. In the middle of this central stanza we see the supreme example of the innocent suffering on behalf of the guilty. 'But he was pierced for our transgressions, he was crushed for our iniquities; the punishment that brought us peace was upon him, and by his wounds we are healed' (v. 5).

All the way through this stanza we see the contrasting pronouns: he/our and we/him. Seven times in the space of three verses this contrast is made. His suffering was physical: 'he took up our infirmities'. It was emotional: he 'carried our sorrows' (v. 4a). His suffering was also spiritual: 'he was pierced for our transgressions' (v. 5a). He died instead of us, and his sufferings brought us peace and healing.

Dr David Yonggi Cho wrote:

During the Korean War many people went to Busan, in Korea's far south. Most people living in Busan, my home then, were very poor, living from day to day. There were not even any jobs to be found.

Because we were desperate for food, we even stole. When American soldiers started hauling coal by freight train from Busan's harbour, many young boys like myself would climb into the filled freight cars like hungry ants. We stole enough coal to sell, wanting to buy enough food and clothes to make it through a small portion of the harsh winter.

One day a group of refugees climbed up on a cargo train to steal coal. Then an American military policeman came running toward them, shouting for them to get down. Frightened, they jumped out of the cargo train.

One small seven-year-old boy was among the group fleeing. He started to run with the rest of the group when he saw some coal that had fallen under the train. He crawled under the train to retrieve that coal. Just as he was about to reach the coal, the train began to move. The people standing nearby shrieked, but no one dared to save that boy and endanger their own lives.

Then one middle-aged man ran near the train. With a burst of his full strength he pushed the boy to safety, clear of the railroad tracks. But the man was no longer safe. In the next moment we heard the cracking of this man's bones as the train's steel wheels tore his body apart. That man had given his life for the young boy. That man was the young boy's father.[36]

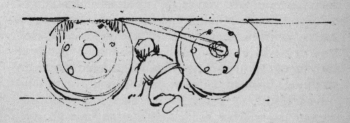

Like the young boy's father Jesus loves us so much that he died instead of us. We are all like sheep who have 'gone astray'. We have all turned to our own way over and over again, but he has taken the punishment on himself. He was exiled from God for us. 'The Lord has laid on him the iniquity of us all' (v. 6).

Fourth contrast: the guilty and the innocent (53:7–9)

He was oppressed and afflicted, yet he did not open his mouth; he was led like a lamb to the slaughter, and as a sheep before her shearers is silent, so he did not open his mouth. By oppression and judgment he was taken away. And who can speak of his descendants? For he was cut off from the land of the living; for the transgression of my people he was stricken. He was assigned a grave with the wicked, and with the rich in his death, though he had done no violence, nor was any deceit in his mouth.

The servant's death was voluntary and undeserved but he knew the importance of what he was doing. There is an extraordinary accuracy about this prophecy. The prophet foresaw the silence of the innocent Jesus.

'He was oppressed and afflicted, yet he did not open his mouth; he was led like a lamb to the slaughter, and as a sheep before her shearers is silent, so he did not open his mouth' (v. 7). His silence impressed his friends. Peter wrote, 'When they hurled insults at him, he did not retaliate; when he suffered, he made no threats. Instead, he entrusted himself to him who judges justly' (1 Pet 2:23). It also impressed his brother James who wrote that the person who controls his tongue perfectly will be able to control everything he does (Jas 3:2).

It even impressed his enemies. 'He [Herod] plied him with many questions, but Jesus gave him no answer' (Lk 23:9). In front of Pilate, 'Jesus gave him no answer' (Jn 19:9). 'And Pilate was amazed' (Mk 15:5). When a man was crucified, the only thing he could hit back with was his mouth. Victims on the cross would curse and swear, like the two thieves either side of Jesus. This was a normal and natural thing to do. Jesus' silence in the face of intense suffering amazed those who watched. When the Roman centurion saw how he died, he said, 'Surely this man was the Son of God!' (Mk 15:39).

Although the kind of death Jesus died was one reserved for criminals, he himself was not guilty: he died under unjust charges. He 'was cut off from the land of the living' not for his own wrongdoing, but for 'the transgression of my people'. It was an inappropriate punishment on human terms, but on God's terms it was the chosen way of salvation.

In verse 9 we see an unusual combination. He died with the wicked and he was assigned a grave with them. The victims of crucifixion would normally have been thrown into Gehenna, the rubbish dump outside Jerusalem. Yet although he was 'assigned a grave with the wicked' he was 'with the rich in his death'.

Thomas Adler, a Romanian doctor, found himself in a labour camp on the Russian frontier during the Second World War. When he escaped, he discovered that almost all his relatives had died in Auschwitz. He finally arrived in Israel with a group of illegal immigrants from Cyprus in April 1948, and ended up among Israeli intellectuals studying Hebrew history and archaeology.

History being always a great hobby of mine, I started devouring books about the Dead Sea scrolls and other literature and finally I started reading the Bible. I discovered all of a sudden that this book became a topic of passionate literature and for a couple of years I read again and again the Old Testament and especially the Prophets and the following verses from Isaiah struck me and embarrassed me. 'He was wounded for our transgressions, bruised for our iniquities. The chastisement of our peace was upon him' and so on. 'For the transgression of *my* people, was he stricken.' I asked myself for months and months what the meaning of these passages was. Why did it say *he* was wounded for *our* transgressions, *he* was bruised for *our* iniquities, by *his* stripes *we* are healed? On one occasion I read again carefully through the verses, starting at Isaiah 52:13 and the whole of chapter 53 and after thorough and careful

thinking I made my mind up that it is *not* the people of
Israel. It must be a person. But who? It must be a
chosen servant of God. The clue came when I read
'and he made his grave with the wicked and with the
rich in his death.' All of a sudden I remembered a story
about a man called Joseph of Arimathea, a rich man,
who offered a new grave for a chosen servant of God.
Next day I purchased a New Testament and I read
carefully through the gospel of Matthew. I understood.
This person, this chosen servant of God, who was numbered with the transgressors and who bore the sin of
many and made intercession for the transgressors could
be only one person—Jesus of Nazareth. The prophet
foresaw with extraordinary accuracy that Joseph of Arimathea would rescue Jesus' body from such a fate and
put him in a rich man's tomb (Jn 19:38–42).[37]

Fifth contrast: tragedy and triumph (53:10–12)

*Yet it was the Lord's will to crush him and cause him to
suffer, and though the Lord makes his life a guilt offering,
he will see his offspring and prolong his days, and the
will of the Lord will prosper in his hand. After the
suffering of his soul, he will see the light of life and be
satisfied; by his knowledge my righteous servant will
justify many, and he will bear their iniquities. Therefore
I will give him a portion among the great, and he will
divide the spoils with the strong, because he poured out
his life unto death, and was numbered with the transgressors. For he bore the sin of many, and made intercession for the transgressors.*

What looked like a defeat was in fact a victory,
planned by Almighty Sovereign God. The prophet
tells us, 'It was the Lord's will to crush him and cause
him to suffer' (v. 10a). As Peter put it on the Day of

Pentecost, 'This man was handed over to you by God's set purpose and foreknowledge; and you, with the help of wicked men, put him to death by nailing him to the cross' (Acts 2:23). This does not excuse those who put him to death, but we do see that it was part of God's plan. As Jesus said in the garden of Gethsemane, 'Not my will, but yours be done' (Lk 22:42).

The cross was not a denial of justice, but the focal point of God's plan to save the world. His sacrificial death was 'a guilt offering' (v. 10). Human sacrifice was never the Old Testament norm. This was a unique event for all time.

What makes this death a triumph? First, 'he will see his offspring' (v. 10). The servant will see the fruit of his labour. As a mother forgets the pains of birth when she sees her baby, so the servant will see the millions of people who will receive new life through his death.

Secondly, 'he will see the light of life' (v. 11). The prophet foresees that he will emerge from his awful task and 'prolong his days' (v. 10). Surely, he gets a glimpse here of the resurrection of Jesus Christ. As Lesslie Newbigin points out, 'The resurrection was not the reversal of a defeat but the manifestation of a victory.'

Thirdly, he will 'be satisfied' (v. 11). Jesus accomplished the work he set out to do, evidenced by his cry on the cross: 'It is finished' (Jn 19:30). The curtain in the temple in Jerusalem was torn from top to bottom, symbolising that it was now possible to have access to God's presence. Jesus completed his task, which was to enable God and human beings to know each other fully and live together in peace once again.

Fourthly, the righteous servant 'will justify many' (v. 11). The word 'righteous' and the word 'justify' have the same root word in Hebrew—*sadeq* (they also have the same root in Greek *dikaios*). Righteousness is about a right relationship with God and our fellow human beings. In principle, the exile is over and our relationship with God is restored. That is what results from justification. It is God's declaration that our sins have been dealt with by the work of the servant and therefore God sees us as righteous: in a right relationship with him. Our guilt has been removed, and death has been conquered, because, as the prophet predicts, 'He will bear their iniquities' (v. 11c).

Fifthly, his achievement will enthrone him as the mighty one. 'Therefore I will give him a portion among the great, and he will divide the spoils with the strong' (v. 12a). God gives a reward to his servant, as if he were sharing with him the spoils of victory. Although Jesus lived in humility, he was raised in glory.

Jesus was 'numbered with transgressors'. He identified with sinners throughout his ministry and ended his life between two thieves. But this servant is both God and man. Paul captures these two sides to the servant in his description of Jesus:

> Who, being in very nature God, did not consider equality with God something to be grasped, but made himself nothing, taking the very nature of a servant, being made in human likeness. And being found in appearance as a man, he humbled himself and became obedient to death—even death on a cross! Therefore God exalted him to the highest place and gave him the name that is above every name, that at the name of Jesus every knee should bow, in heaven and on earth and under the earth, and

every tongue confess that Jesus Christ is Lord, to the glory of God the Father (Phil 2:6–11).

This is all good news. Everything that follows in the book of Isaiah is a result of what the servant is predicted to achieve in this chapter. Our response should be one of amazement, love and dedication to Jesus.

John Williams used to work for a commodity firm. He enjoyed reading and had a permanent order with his bookseller to be sent one copy of all Penguin books published in the 'classic' series. One of the books that arrived for him was a copy of a new translation of the four gospels prepared by Dr E. V. Rieu. He took the book for reading as he travelled to work.

One day he had finished work in the office and then gone to help at a youth club, catching a late train home. He settled into a corner seat, opened the book and saw that he had reached Luke's account of the crucifixion.

There were two other men in the compartment, one was an Englishman and the other an American. The Englishman suddenly fell on to the floor of the compartment and had a convulsive fit. The American leapt to help him, loosened his tie and put his handkerchief into the Englishman's mouth to keep him from biting his tongue.

The American said to John Williams, 'I'm awfully sorry; but this happens several times each week. You see, we fought in the Korean war together, and I was wounded and left in no man's land; and this Englishman came and carried me to safety. Just as we were arriving at a safe position a shell landed beside us, and the next thing we knew was that we were in hospital.

I was invalided out of the army back to America when I heard that the Englishman would never get better. I left my job, broke off my engagement and came to England to look after him. You see, *he did that for me. There is nothing that I cannot do for him.*' The train had arrived at the next station. By that time the Englishman was much better and he and the American got out. John Williams was left alone in the compartment of the train as it swayed through the dark night. He continued to read the story of the crucifixion with a voice ringing in his ears: '*He did that for me; there is nothing that I cannot do for him.*' Suddenly he closed the book, knelt in the compartment of the train and gave his life to Christ.[38]

Recently, I received a long letter from a woman who was doing the Alpha course at our church. She described her life of sin and suffering, involving alcoholism, sexual abuse, drugs, truancy, divorce, domestic violence and suicide attempts. There followed pages on how she had tried to sort her life out through things like hypnotism and psychotherapy. Then one day she received a telephone call from someone who had done the previous Alpha course.

He had found what I had been searching for all these years . . . All those years of feeling utterly desolate, utterly unclean and ashamed, riddled with guilt and not believing I deserved forgiveness but longing for it, were all soon to end. I had been living my life in a dark hole, I was carrying a great weight on my shoulders . . . God has forgiven me . . . because Jesus Christ has removed all my sin when he suffered crucifixion and died for us all . . . That burden has gone from my shoulders and I am filled with great hope, joy, excitement and love and all I want to do is to serve Christ in whatever form he chooses.

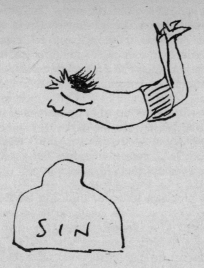

When we have experienced the love of God we will want everyone else to have that same experience. Paul writes, 'For Christ's love compels us, because we are convinced that one died for all . . . that those who live should no longer live for themselves but for him who died for them and was raised again' (2 Cor 5:14–15).

The central message of revival is one of good news. It is a message about the suffering servant Jesus and, in particular, his life, death and resurrection. Raniero Cantalamessa puts it like this:

The point is Jesus Christ. Whenever the Holy Spirit comes in a new and fresh way upon the Church, Jesus Christ comes alive. Jesus Christ is set at the centre. He is proclaimed in Spirit and power, which means in the power of the Spirit.

This is the first model of evangelisation and if we want to

re-evangelise our secularised, modern world, this is how
we must start: Jesus Christ in the centre, Jesus Christ as
Lord. This is, I repeat, the model of any evangelisation.
We must start by presenting to modern man the person of
Jesus, or better still, by helping modern mankind to come
into a personal relationship with Jesus.

What the world needs is to have a personal relationship
with Jesus as Saviour and Lord. We have developed such
a huge heritage of doctrine that we don't realise that this
is too much for a person who does not yet know Jesus,
who doesn't understand who Jesus is.

We must proclaim Jesus as Lord and Saviour, helping
people to grasp what it means to have Jesus as their
Saviour—not in a theoretical way, but that every day
they have a Saviour, someone who will lift them from
the fatigue of the day, of their sin, and their mistakes,
and who renews them. He saves us. When you proclaim this living, crucified and risen Jesus, something
always happens.[39]

This is the initial distinguishing mark of the Spirit of
God in revival according to Jonathan Edwards.

When the operation is such as to raise their esteem of that
Jesus who was born of the Virgin, and was crucified without the gates of Jerusalem; and seems more to confirm and
establish their minds in the truth of what the gospel
declares to us of his being the Son of God, and the Saviour
of man; it is a sure sign that it is from the Spirit of God.

The Spirit . . . works in them an admiring, delightful
sense of the excellency of Jesus Christ; representing him
as the chief among ten thousand, and altogether lovely,
and makes him precious to the soul.[40]

Thus we read of the 1858 revival in the USA: 'Never
was the name of Christ so honoured, never so often

mentioned, never so precious to the believer. Never was such ardent love to him expressed.'[41]

Without Jesus we would be lost. Revival comes to individual men and women when they understand what he has done, receive the 'benefits of his passion' and respond by giving up their lives to his service. No revival can be a true revival unless this message is central. Dr Martyn Lloyd-Jones wrote: 'Revival, above everything else, is a glorification of the Lord Jesus Christ, the Son of God. It is the restoration of Him to the centre of the life of the church.'[42] Like Paul, when he went to Corinth, we should determine to know nothing except 'Jesus Christ and him crucified' (1 Cor 2:2).

6

What Is the Vision?

Isaiah 54

At the age of twelve, William Carey (1761–1834) finished his education in Northamptonshire and became a shoemaker. At the age of fourteen he was led to Christ by a fellow cobbler. From then on, as a member of the Baptist church, his one burning desire was to know Jesus Christ and to make him known throughout the world. However, up to this point British churches had done little in terms of overseas mission and some Christians tried to dampen his enthusiasm.

".. go ye and make me a coffee instead"

An older minister said to him, when he stood to speak of his vision, 'Sit down, young man . . . if the Lord wants to convert the heathen, he can do it without your help.'

In 1792 Carey wrote a paper, the full title of which was: 'An enquiry into the obligations of Christians to use means for the conversion of the heathens. In which the religious state of the different nations of the world, the success of former undertakings, and the practicability of further undertakings, are considered, by William Carey.'

He pointed out that Jesus commissioned his disciples to 'go', and that this 'laid them under obligation to disperse themselves into every country in the habitable globe, and preach to all the inhabitants, without exception or limitation'. This flew in the face of the then accepted view of the Protestant churches that there was no mandate for foreign mission after the period of the first apostles. In the second section of the book he reviewed former undertakings, looking at men like Justin Martyr in the second century and John Calvin, who had said that the great commission had no statute of limitation: 'Go ye', means 'you' and 'now'! In the third section he surveyed the present state of the world and finally called the church to fervent and united prayer. He ended by writing, 'Surely, it is worthwhile to lay ourselves out with all our might in promoting the cause and the Kingdom of Christ.'

In May 1792 Carey preached a most significant and electrifying sermon. His text was Isaiah 54:2–3. His biographer, Timothy George, records that

Carey took the prophet's words addressed to ancient Israel in a time of distress and applied it to the church in his day. Indeed, there was much in his own experience of the church to confirm the sullen image Isaiah paints: a barren widow, bereft of her husband, with no offspring to give hope or cheer. Yet the prophet calls for rejoicing, not lamentation; for celebration, not sorrow. The promise is this: God is about to restore the church and his work will be extraordinary and wonderful . . . there is to be an enlargement in God's people, a bringing in of others on the right and the left, a winning of the Gentiles who are yet to be included in the covenant of grace. The burden of the sermon came to a crescendo in a summarising couplet: 'Expect great things [from God]. Attempt great things [for God].'[43]

What could one small body of Baptists, in a backwater of Northamptonshire, do to evangelise the world? A hundred years later F. W. Farrar, Canon of Westminster Abbey and afterwards Dean of Canterbury, said of those who mocked, 'Those who in that day sneered that England had sent a cobbler to convert the world were the direct linear descendants of those who sneered in Palestine 2000 years ago, "Is not this the Carpenter?"'

William Carey is now universally recognised as the father of modern missions. He himself went to India for forty years. He translated the New Testament into Bengali and Sanskrit. He had a vision to preach Christ to the world and to that end he proclaimed the gospel and campaigned against the evils in society. He had a significant impact on the conversion to Jesus Christ of people all over the world. In the West, this reputation for being the 'father of modern missions' came about not simply because of his remarkable translation work but also because he was the author of ideas and philosophies by which future missions were to be guided. As a result of his thinking missionaries reached out into previously unknown corners of the world.

The background to Isaiah 54 and 55 is, again, the exile. Israel is compared to a woman who feels deserted, robbed of her husband, children and home. But these are the very three things God is going to restore to her. How is this possible? The keynote of chapters 54 and 55 is 'response'. We need to respond to what God has done through his servant in chapter 52:10—53:12. The servant has removed sin and has made possible fruitfulness, peace and righteousness. There is a twofold task. First, it involves restoring the survivors of Israel (chapter 54) and, secondly, bringing God's truth to the Gentiles (chapter 55).

The command to grow and to go (vv. 1–3)

'Sing, O barren woman, you who never bore a child; burst into song, shout for joy, you who were never in labour; because more are the children of the desolate woman than of her who has a husband,' says the Lord. 'Enlarge the place of your tent, stretch your tent curtains wide, do not hold back; lengthen your cords, strengthen your stakes. For you will spread out to the right and to the left; your descendants will dispossess nations and settle in their desolate cities.'

For a woman to be barren was a mark of shame in ancient Israel. But now Israel is commanded to sing and rejoice (v. 1a), because God will give her so many children (v. 1b) that she will need a bigger home. The illustration used is that of a Bedouin tent (v. 2), which was relatively simple to enlarge. It involved three tasks, all of which were part of the traditional role of women in the ancient world.

First, new sections were added: 'stretch your tent curtains wide' (v. 2a). Extra skins needed to be incorporated into the tent. Secondly, longer cords were required: 'lengthen your cords' (v. 2b). Thirdly, more substantial stakes were needed to hold the weight: 'strengthen your stakes' (v. 2b). In other words, more breadth was needed so that the tent would be of a sufficient size to accommodate a large family. More depth was required so that the tent would be strong enough to withstand any storm. Finally, expansion needed to take place in expectation of future growth. The expression, 'For you will spread out to the right and to the left' (v. 3a) means spreading out in every direction.

God longs for the church today to expand and to grow. First, we need to build strong church bases—'strengthen your stakes' (v. 2). We can strengthen our love and devotion to God through prayer, through studying the Bible, through building home groups and running training courses and every other method which helps to strengthen the church. But we do not wait until this has been completed before we go out.

Secondly, we are called to have more children (v. 1). The church today has inherited Israel's God-given calling: to be a light and a blessing to the rest of the world. Isaiah clearly foresees growth in the numbers of God's people, yet much of the church does not reproduce. Church growth expert, Dr Peter Wagner, has pointed out that planting new churches in areas which have few Christians is one of the most effective strategies for evangelism.

> Church growth is usually rapid where not only individuals are being won to Christ, but where simultaneously churches are being multiplied . . . In most places in the world, there is a direct correlation between new congregational starts and the rate of church growth . . . Time and again research has confirmed that planting new churches is the most effective evangelistic methodology known under heaven.[44]

We can trust God's promise and rejoice (v. 1), knowing that as we co-operate with God, more people will be added to his church.

Thirdly, we are required to have a wide vision (v. 3). The gospel of Jesus Christ is public truth for the entire world. The 1974 Lausanne Covenant, produced by the International Congress on World Evangelisation, included a significant definition of evangelism. 'To evangelise,' it stated, 'is to spread the good news that Jesus Christ died for our sins and was raised from the dead according to the Scriptures, and that as the reigning Lord he now offers the forgiveness of sins and the liberating gift of the Spirit to all who repent and believe. . . . The results of evangelism include obedience to Christ, incorporation into his church and responsible service in the world.'[45]

The potential is vast. Although one third of the world's population professes the name of Christ, millions have not even heard about Christ. There is a desperate need. We who are Christians are entrusted with the best news in all the world. We cannot simply sit around and selfishly enjoy it. We need to get the message out.

All these three take place at the same time. Bishop Lesslie Newbigin points out that it is often

> taken for granted that the missionary obligation is one that has to be met *after* the needs of the home have been fully met; that existing gains have to be thoroughly consolidated before we go further afield; that the world-wide church has to be built up with the same sort of prudent calculations of resources and costs as is expected of any business enterprise.

He continues:

> Must we not contrast this with the sort of strategy that the New Testament reveals, which seems to be a sort of determination to stake out God's claim to the whole world at once, without expecting that one area should be fully worked out before the next is claimed? Thus our Lord forbids his disciples to stay and argue with those who do not receive them, but tells them to shake off the dust of their feet for a testimony and go on. And Paul's missionary planning leaps to the end of the known world, urging him forward from each field of work to the next, not when the church has been fully built up but when the gospel has been fully preached.[46]

Pastoral care and building the church happen as the church fulfils the commission of Jesus. Again, Bishop Lesslie Newbigin puts it like this:

Participation in Christ means participation in his mission to the world, and therefore true pastoral care, true training in the Christian life, and true use of the means of grace will be precisely in and for the discharge of this missionary task. Speaking in terms of the experience of the village church in India as I know it, this will mean that a newly baptised congregation will not be trained *first* in churchmanship and *then* in missionary responsibility to neighbouring villages. It will receive its training in churchmanship precisely in the discharge of its missionary responsibility. 'Consolidation' will not be the alternative to advance: on the contrary, advance will be the method of consolidation.[47]

Reaching out to the world around us is not 'empire building', but, rather, it is a response to God's call to see the kingdom of God coming in power. This is not something any church can achieve on its own, but as churches of different denominations across the world work together, it has recently become a real possibility.

The final statement at the 1966 Berlin Congress on Evangelism included the words, 'Our goal is nothing short of the evangelisation of the human race in this generation.' Billy Graham said on that occasion, 'The evangelistic harvest is always urgent. The destiny of men and of nations is always being decided. Every generation is crucial; every generation is strategic. But we are not responsible for the past generation, and we cannot bear full responsibility for the next one. However, we do have our generation! God will hold us responsible at the Judgement Seat of Christ for how well we fulfilled our responsibilities and took advantage of our opportunities.'[48]

This task is not the exclusive calling of 'evangelists' or the clergy; it is for all God's people. Pope John Paul

II, in an address given in 1990 at Vera Cruz, Mexico, said, 'The work of proclaiming the gospel to all nations is a responsibility which falls to all and to each one of those who by the Lord's grace are and call themselves Christians.'[49] Billy Graham has said, 'I believe one of the greatest priorities of the Church today is to mobilise the laity to do the work of evangelism.'[50]

The importance of getting our priorities right (vv. 4–10)

'Do not be afraid; you will not suffer shame. Do not fear disgrace; you will not be humiliated. You will forget the shame of your youth and remember no more the reproach of your widowhood. For your Maker is your husband—the Lord Almighty is his name—the Holy One of Israel is your Redeemer; he is called the God of all the earth. The Lord will call you back as if you were a wife deserted and distressed in spirit—a wife who married young, only to be rejected,' says your God. 'For a brief moment I aban-doned you, but with deep compassion I will bring you back. In a surge of anger I hid my face from you for a moment but with everlasting kindness I will have compassion on you,' says the Lord your Redeemer.

'To me this is like the days of Noah, when I swore that the waters of Noah would never again cover the earth. So now I have sworn not to be angry with you, never to rebuke you again. Though the mountains be shaken and the hills be removed, yet my unfailing love for you will not be shaken nor my covenant of peace be removed,' says the Lord, who has compassion on you.

The prophet moves from the picture of the growing family back to the analogy of marriage. If in the first section the key concept was fruitfulness, here it is 'peace' (v. 10).

The section starts with the most common command in the Bible—'Do not be afraid' (v. 4), which appears 366 times. The vision is such a vast one that we might be fearful, but God says we need not be. We may have complete confidence because he promises that the history of past ineffectiveness and weakness is utterly behind us: 'Do not fear disgrace; you will not be humiliated. You will forget the shame of your youth and remember no more the reproach of your widow-hood' (v. 4).

We also need not fear because 'your Maker is your husband' (v. 5). As we have seen, Isaiah's analogy of our relationship with God being like that of a wife with a husband is a common one in the Bible (eg Hosea 1–3; Isaiah 62:5; Jeremiah 2:2; Ezekiel 16:8; Mark 2:19). The prophets proclaimed that Israel had been an unfaithful wife and had gone after other gods.

However, God gives three reassurances. First, he will restore their relationship with him: 'For a brief moment I abandoned you, but with deep compassion I will bring you back' (v. 7). The brief period of alienation is contrasted with the greatness of God's love and reconciliation—the period of exile is insignificant compared with the immensity of the love with which he will take his people back.

Secondly, his kindness is endless and everlasting compared to a short burst of anger at his people's sin: '"In a surge of anger I hid my face from you for a moment, but with everlasting kindness I will have compassion on you," says the Lord your Redeemer' (v. 8).

Thirdly, there is a permanence to his love: 'To me

this is like the days of Noah, when I swore that the waters of Noah would never again cover the earth. So now I have sworn not to be angry with you, never to rebuke you again' (v. 9). God made a covenant with Israel after the flood. Likewise, he promises here never to punish Israel in the same way again. He will make an eternal covenant of love and peace (v. 10).

Once again, this is all dependent on the work of the servant, for 'the punishment that brought us peace was upon him' (53:5). The Hebrew word for peace, *shalom*, means well-being of every kind.

We have seen earlier how in the exile Israel went after other gods. Now God calls his people away from these adulterous relationships back into an intimate relationship with him. The temptation to go after other gods is an ever-present one. Sometimes this is fairly obvious, such as sacrificing our lives for money, sex or power. At other times, the idolatry is more subtle. I heard one American church leader speak about the temptation to make our first priority something other than God. He said that he was sometimes tempted to put his ministry above his relationship with God. He described it as a man falling in love with his wife's

twin sister. She might look almost identical to his wife and it might 'feel so right' to make her the priority, but it would still be an adulterous relationship. There does, of course, exist an appropriate love for our ministry, but our primary love should be for our Maker, who is our husband. Nothing, not even death, can rob us of that everlasting relationship.

The promise of victory (vv. 11–17)

'O afflicted city, lashed by storms and not comforted, I will build you with stones of turquoise, your foundations with sapphires. I will make your battlements of rubies, your gates of sparkling jewels, and all your walls of precious stones. All your sons will be taught by the Lord, and great will be your children's peace. In righteousness you will be established: Tyranny will be far from you; you will have nothing to fear. Terror will be far removed; it will not come near you. If anyone does attack you, it will not be my doing; whoever attacks you will surrender to you.

'See, it is I who created the blacksmith who fans the coals into flame and forges a weapon fit for its work. And it is I who have created the destroyer to work havoc; no weapon forged against you will prevail, and you will refute every tongue that accuses you. This is the heritage of the servants of the Lord, and this is their vindication from me,' declares the Lord.

In the third section of this chapter, the prophet moves from the picture of the family and the husband to a picture of the home and the city. In this section the key word is 'righteousness' (v. 14) and its primary reference point is the rebuilding of Jerusalem which was to take place under the direction of Nehemiah. This rebuilding of the walls of Jerusalem is often taken to represent the rebuilding of the church. First, God promises that the glory of Jerusalem will be restored: '"O afflicted city, lashed by storms and not comforted, I will build you with stones of turquoise, your foundations with sapphires. I will make your battlements of rubies, your gates of sparkling jewels, and all your walls of precious stones"' (vv. 11–12). This is an image of dazzling splendour, a city that reflects God's glory.

Secondly, God promises wonderful privileges for the people of that city: 'All your sons will be taught by the Lord, and great will be your children's peace' (v. 13). The servant had said, 'He wakens me morning by morning, wakens my ear to listen like one being taught' (Is 50:4). Now all God's people will be 'taught by the Lord'. They will be given the skills required for rebuilding and God will show them what to do.

Thirdly, God promises his protection (vv. 14–17): 'In righteousness you will be established' (v. 14a). The work of the servant described in chapter 53 was to 'justify many' (53:11). The acceptance of God's people is complete and they are righteous in his sight. God promises his complete protection.

He promises that 'tyranny will be far from you' (v. 14a). 'Tyranny' in this context refers to the disturbance of society from within. Today, one of the main threats to the church is the internal threat of disunity. God promises his protection from this. Secondly, he promises that 'Terror will be far removed; it will not come near you' (v. 14b). 'Terror' is an assault from outside. Again, God is sovereign and no attack can ultimately succeed against the people of the Lord who will be strong enough to overcome (v. 15).

God is sovereign over humans, their knowledge and skills, and all they may create (v. 16). Even the mechanical device is under his control. He is also sovereign over the intention behind the attack (v. 16c)—'I . . . created the destroyer to work havoc.' This is a strong Hebrew way of saying that God permits, overrules and brings good out of evil. Finally, he is sovereign over the outcome: 'No weapon forged against you will prevail, and you will refute every tongue that accuses you' (v. 17). The fire may burn but it will not consume.

Up to this point the word 'servant' has been used in the singular. Now the prophet refers to 'the servants of the Lord' (v. 17c). The saving work of 'the servant' creates 'servants' who will be 'vindicated', which means delivered, given salvation. Literally, it means 'made righteous'. These servants' status before God could not be more honourable.

Recently, in a small way, I had an experience of God's sovereignty. I went with a team to speak at some Alpha conferences in Canada and North America and almost everything that could go wrong did go wrong. It seemed as though we were under attack and as if the devil did not want Alpha to take off in America. Our resource materials were impounded by customs and they would not release them in spite of the fact that the duty had been paid. We paid twice, but even then they did not release them. On the opening day of the conference in Toronto nothing had arrived and the conference delegates naturally wanted to read the books and view the material first. Some 500 people were anxiously asking for the resources. Finally they arrived at the end of the first day.

That night my hotel room was burgled. Among the personal possessions stolen were my wallet, my Bible (with thirteen years of notes in it), my Filofax with notes for the talks, my diary and address book and my USA papers, including my driving licence and passport.

So just before the conference began we had to make frantic phone calls to the police, and to my bank in England. Most serious was the lack of a passport. I was supposed to be leading another conference in Washington DC on the Tuesday and Wednesday of the following week. The burglary was discovered on Thursday. Ahead was the weekend, and Monday was Labour Day when everything is closed in North America. It was impossible to get a new passport in Toronto so I had to fly to Ottawa on Friday morning. As I was not speaking on the second morning (Friday) of the conference in Toronto I arranged to fly to Ottawa in the morning and fly back by 2pm for the afternoon session.

When I reached the passport office in Ottawa, the man at the desk said that my papers had not arrived from Toronto. He also had no information from England and my name was not even on his computer. I had to go out, get more photos taken and I had to pay again. When I came back they said it was very unlikely that they would be able to issue a passport since they had not yet received the necessary information from England. By then there was only ninety minutes to go until my return flight.

I decided to ring England. They said the nearest phone was in the Royal Bank about five minutes away. I raced over there and found an assistant there called Miriam and showed her a copy of *Alpha News*, with my picture and the dates of the conferences. I told her what had happened to all my possessions. She allowed me to make a reverse charge call to England. While I was on the phone to England she was eagerly reading the *Alpha News*! Eventually, I got through to my wife and urged her to ask everyone we knew who had any influence to ring the High Commission in Ottawa.

I then ran back to the Consulate and again asked to see the High Commissioner, Sir Nicholas Bayne. The staff sent me round to the other side of the building. I was told at the reception desk that I had come to the wrong place to see the High Commissioner and should go back to the passport office. So I ran back round to the passport office. By this time the security guard, who had to check in my details whenever I entered was fed up and was making it harder and harder for me to get back in. There was thirty-five minutes to go. When I arrived again at the desk the man there said that they would do all they could to issue a passport. The High Commissioner was now aware of the situation. I said: 'Have you had any phone calls?' He said: 'Yes, we have even had a bishop ringing!' I was told that the passport would be ready in ten minutes, but they said I would also need a visa from the US Embassy.

The US Embassy was five minutes away and there was a long queue. I told the man at the door about the urgency of the situation. He said all I could do was join the line. Suddenly, I saw an empty window with a woman standing behind the counter. I went up to her and explained the situation. She said, 'Right. I don't think you need a visa, but I'll sort it out. Go and collect your passport so that you don't waste any time.' I raced back to the British Consulate. By this time the security man downstairs had had enough and said it was the last time he would let me in. I went up, got the passport and raced back to the US Embassy. They told me they had sorted it out and that I did not need a visa.

We drove as fast as we could to the airport, but we just missed the midday flight. There was no 1pm flight, so I transferred airlines. I was put on standby, but told that I had little chance of catching the 1pm flight unless I transferred to Club Class. I said I would transfer. They said I needed to pay by credit card. But I only had cash. I had to go back to the office downstairs to pay by cash. Eventually, at ten to one I was told I was on the plane. I arrived back for the next session of the conference exactly on time.

Meanwhile, a massive amount of prayer had ascended to the heavens! There was a prayer meeting at Toronto and another at my home church in London which had heard of the crisis. Then there were two Christian men who had met me at Ottawa airport and who had prayed constantly. These two men, who stayed with me throughout the morning, asked me on the way to the Consulate about the conference I was leading in Toronto. It turned out that they had been at a home group leaders' meeting the night before and they had felt that God was calling their church to reach out in evangelism and had asked God to show them what they should do. When I told them about the Alpha course the Holy Spirit came upon them abruptly there and then in the car. The driver was so excited and so physically moved that I became anxious for our safety on the road! I started to wonder, too, whether God had taken me away from the conference in Toronto simply in order that I could speak to these two men in Ottawa. God in his sovereignty was bringing good out of the situation.

On the plane back to Toronto, I wrote to the two men thanking them for the amazing way in which they had supported me, and saying that I would send them all the Alpha material they needed to start their own course. I also wrote to Miriam, at the Royal Bank, sending her a copy of *Alpha News* and also a copy of *Questions of Life*. And thirdly, I sent a letter to the High Commissioner, Sir Nicholas Bayne, again enclosing *Questions of Life*! It struck me afterwards that the whole episode was spiritual warfare. It was an illustration, admittedly trivial in some ways, of the kind of battle that takes place in a far greater and more important way all the time in the church on earth. In all these things God is sovereign and no weapon formed against us can prevail.

On a more serious note, although God promises ultimate protection and victory, he does not promise that there will be no attacks or problems (v. 15). In the sixteenth century, Cranmer, Ridley, Latimer and many others were burned at the stake. Jonathan Edwards, who spearheaded the New England revival of the 1730s, was ultimately compelled to resign from the church which had been so blessed by the revival. He wrote, 'Many scoffed at and ridiculed it; and some compared what we called conversion to certain distempers.'[51] John Pollock records in his biography of John Wesley how 'Methodists had windows broken and houses, shops and workshops shamelessly looted; they were beaten and splattered with mud'.[52]

It is almost invariably the case that revival will be opposed. It was true of Jesus' own ministry, like the prophets before him and the apostles after him. It was true of the Reformation, the Puritan and Methodist revivals, the Great Awakening, the ministry of Finney, Spurgeon, Moody and many others, the Welsh revival and the modern Pentecostal movement. Arthur Wallis wrote, 'If we find a revival that is not spoken against, we had better look again to ensure that it is a revival.'[53]

Christian faith is opposed in many different ways in today's society, even though not all Christians are obviously 'persecuted' on a regular basis. As Paul wrote, 'We are hard pressed on every side but not crushed; perplexed but not in despair; persecuted but not abandoned; struck down but not destroyed' (2 Cor 4:8–9).

Nevertheless, he went on, 'We do not lose heart, though outwardly we are wasting away, yet inwardly we are being renewed day by day. For our light and momentary troubles are achieving for us an eternal glory that far outweighs them all. So we fix our eyes not on what is seen, but on what is unseen. For what is seen is temporary, but what is unseen is eternal' (2 Cor 4:16–18).

The reason for Paul's confidence is the resurrection of Jesus. Paul writes, 'With that same Spirit of faith we also believe and therefore speak, because we know that the one who raised the Lord Jesus from the dead will also raise us with Jesus and present us with you in his presence' (2 Cor 4:14). It is only because of the resurrection of Jesus that we can be confident that 'no weapon formed against us can succeed'.

God's vision is so often bigger than our own. It is a worldwide one. We should not settle for anything less. We thank God for local revivals and national revivals but we should not be satisfied until we see a worldwide revival. This will stem from his love which is greater even than that between a husband and wife. Not only does he desire to bring this vision about, he has the power to do so. He is the sovereign Lord who ultimately will not allow anything to stand in his way. As Paul put it: 'In all things God works for the good of those who love him and are called according to his purpose' (Rom 8:28). Our vision should be to 'go and make disciples of all nations' (Mt 28:19). As the Pope has said, 'The Church's vitality is measured by her missionary and evangelising dimension and thrust.'[54] This is not an option but a duty: our response to Jesus' command. Let us once again 'expect great things from God and attempt great things for him'.

"Father, ambitious as it is, if possible, I'd like to give you a third of these toffees"

7

What Is the Invitation?

Isaiah 55

Billy Graham has often said, 'The Bible is one long invitation to come to God.' In the opening chapters of Genesis, after Adam's rejection of God's perfect plan, God calls to Adam with an anguished cry, full of love and anger, 'Where are you?' The book of Revelation ends with the invitation from the Spirit and the Bride who say, 'Come!' Jesus often invited people: 'Come to me' (Mt 11:28); 'Come to the wedding banquet' (Mt 22:4); 'Come to me and drink' (Jn 7:37). In this chapter God once again issues an invitation. The word 'come' appears four times in the first verse.

The invitation is urgent and universal. It is addressed to those who are unsatisfied. In this chapter Isaiah gives four reasons why we should come.

God alone can satisfy the hunger in our hearts (vv. 1–3a)

Come, all you who are thirsty, come to the waters; and you who have no money, come, buy and eat! Come, buy wine and milk without money and without cost. Why spend money on what is not bread, and your labour on what does not satisfy? Listen, listen to me, and eat what is good, and your soul will delight in the richest of fare. Give ear and come to me; hear me, that your soul may live.

Babylon was a centre of commerce. Israel, in exile, was becoming a nation of traders, so God addressed them in a language they would understand: that of the marketplace. The opening verses echo the cries of those selling their wares, and the message is this: material things do not satisfy. Making money does not bring contentment, but leaves a sense of longing. The Greek philosopher Plato once compared human beings to leaky jars. No matter how much one pours into a leaky container, it will never be completely filled. Without God we too are always partly empty, and experience a lack of fulfilment and happiness. The novelist Alexander Solzhenitsyn wrote, 'Our life consists not in the pursuit of material success . . . Material laws alone do not explain our life or give it direction . . . .'[55]

Marxism recognises this feeling of dissatisfaction and asserts that when the 'revolution' comes this

sense of emptiness (which, it claims, is the direct result of capitalism) will disappear. But in those parts of the world where the revolution has come, the sense of alienation and dissatisfaction has remained, and has often even increased.

The atheist philosopher, Jean-Paul Sartre, persistently pointed out the disconcerting truth that we cannot find happiness in anything human or created. He noticed the innate human desire to deny our inability to find satisfaction in the world: we cannot bear to live with the idea that fulfilment will permanently elude us. In a famous line he wrote, 'Man is absurd but he must grimly act as if he were not.'

This hunger for meaning and purpose in life can only be satisfied by God. The psychiatrist Paul Tournier declared, 'Let us be the first to discover what modern man is seeking. He is thirsty for God . . . Everybody today is searching for an answer to those problems to which science pays no attention, the problem of their destiny, the mystery of evil, the question of death.'

"what d'you mean, why am I alive? Stick to the Curriculum"

C. S. Lewis identified a desire that no natural happiness will satisfy. He said that the things of beauty after which we chase, are not 'the real thing'. They are not beauty itself. They are not 'the ultimate reward'. They 'are only the scent of a flower we have not found, the echo of a tune we have not heard, news from a country we have never yet visited'.[56] That which we think will bring us continual pleasure and happiness only leaves us as victims wanting more. When we are fifteen years old, we want to be sixteen; when we acquire a car or a house, we want a bigger or better one.

The trouble with idols is that they do not deliver the life they promise. For example, however much money people make, they will never be satisfied. Elvis Presley, in his heyday, grossed $100 million in two years of stardom. He had three jets, two Cadillacs, a Rolls Royce, a Lincoln Continental, Buick and Chrysler station wagons, a jeep, a dune buggy, a converted bus and three motor cycles. His favourite car was his 1960 Cadillac limousine. The top was covered with pearl-white Naugahide. The body was sprayed with forty coats of a specially prepared paint which included crushed diamonds and fish scales. Nearly all the metal trim was plated with eighteen carat gold. Inside the car there were two gold-plated telephones, a gold vanity case containing a gold electric razor and gold hair clippers, an electric shoe-buffer, a gold-plated television, a record player, an amplifier, air-conditioning, and a refrigerator. He had everything. Yet he was unfulfilled. These things do not fill the aching void. They always leave us wanting more. God asks, 'Why spend money on what is not bread, and your labour on what does not satisfy?' (55:2a) He suggests an alternative: 'Come to me' (v. 3).

First, the invitation is to all who are thirsty. It is to those who recognise their need and humbly say to God, 'Lord, I need you to come and fill me.'

Secondly, the offer is free. It is to 'you who have no money'. Shops are not interested in people with no money. Yet this shopkeeper says, 'You can have my best bread and wine, and it is absolutely free.' They are free because, in fact, they have already been paid for. The shopkeeper has paid for them himself! Similarly, many of God's greatest blessings are free, but only because the servant has paid for them himself. And the cost was very great—nothing less than his own lifeblood (see Isaiah 53). That is why Isaiah 55 follows close on the heels of the substitutionary death of the servant of the Lord.

Thirdly, those who come are deeply satisfied (vv. 2b–3a). To those who come he promises that 'your soul will delight in the richest of fare' (v. 2b). God does not offer us junk food, but a feast. As hymn-writer John Newton wrote:

Solid joys and lasting treasure,
None but Zion's children know.

Billy Graham, in his autobiography, recounts an incident in his life when he and his wife, Ruth, were on an
island in the Caribbean. 'One of the wealthiest men in
the world asked us to come to his lavish home for
lunch. He was seventy-five years old, and throughout
the entire meal he seemed close to tears.

'"I am the most miserable man in the world," he
said. "Out there is my yacht. I can go anywhere I
want to. I have my private plane, my helicopters. I
have everything I want to make me happy. And yet
I'm miserable as hell."'

Billy and his wife talked and prayed with the man,
trying to point him to Christ. That afternoon they
were visited by the local pastor, who was also
seventy-five. He was full of enthusiasm and love for
Christ and for others. He said, 'I don't have two
pounds to my name, but I'm the happiest man on
this island.'

Billy Graham goes on, '"Who do you think is the
richer man?", I asked Ruth after he left. We both knew
the answer.'[57]

God has a purpose for our lives (vv. 3b–5)

*I will make an everlasting covenant with you, my faithful
love promised to David. See, I have made him a witness to
the peoples, a leader and commander of the peoples. Surely
you will summon nations you know not, and nations that
do not know you will hasten to you, because of the Lord
your God, the Holy One of Israel, for he has endowed you
with splendour.*

God's blessings were never intended to be enjoyed selfishly. They were to overflow to others. We can't offer to others what we have not received ourselves. But when we have enjoyed a blessing, we need to pass it on.

God once made this promise to David: ' . . . I will raise up your offspring to succeed you . . . I will establish the throne of his kingdom for ever. I will be his father, and he shall be my son . . . my love will never be taken away from him . . . your house and your kingdom shall endure for ever before me; your throne shall be established for ever' (2 Sam 7:12–16). What was promised to David is also promised to Israel. But just as David failed to fulfil his calling because of sin, so did Israel—with one exception. There was one true Israelite, but only one: the servant of the Lord. Paul sees this passage as referring primarily to Jesus (Acts 13:34).

David was a 'type' of the Messiah. He was *a* leader, but Jesus is *the* leader. Jesus is 'great David's greater son'. He is the 'Pioneer' (Heb 12: 2, RSV). He opens up the road for far more followers than David ever had. So through 'the servant' these promises apply to all the other servants: you and me. What David was to Israel, Israel was called to be to the world, or to the 'nations' (v. 5). Now this is our calling (1 Pet 2:9). The language used shows the extensive nature of the call. It is a call to go to the ends of the earth, far beyond the relatively small known world of the sixth century BC. For this calling he has equipped us: 'For he has endowed [us] with splendour' (v. 5). We are called to reach out not only to our communities but also to every nation in the world.

The greatness of God's love and mercy (vv. 6–9)

Seek the Lord while he may be found; call on him while he is near. Let the wicked forsake his way and the evil man his thoughts. Let him turn to the Lord, and he will have mercy on him, and to our God, for he will freely pardon. 'For my thoughts are not your thoughts, neither are your ways my ways,' declares the Lord. 'As the heavens are higher than the earth, so are my ways higher than your ways and my thoughts than your thoughts.'

We need to grasp our spiritual opportunities. They will not last for ever. 'Seek the Lord while he may be found; call on him while he is near' (v. 6). There are times when we sense God's presence. He may speak to us through a friend, or through some momentous event like a wedding or the birth of a baby. He may wait patiently until we are ready to listen. Or we may find him in our suffering: through an accident, the break-up of our marriage, or through bereavement. In a strange way, we know that he is near. We need to make the most of these opportunities. They may never come again. This equally applies to churches. There are times when God manifests his presence, inviting us to respond to him. We need to seize these opportunities whenever they present themselves.

Wheaton College, Illinois, is a liberal arts college with strong Christian roots. On the evening of Sunday 19th March 1995, over 800 people assembled to worship. There was a time of repentance, confession, weeping and an outpouring of God's grace. It continued until 6am. At 9.30pm the following evening, 1,000 gathered in the chapel, when many people brought forward items that were disturbing their fellowship with God, such as books, magazines and videos. After a time of confession and repentance, God poured his peace and joy on them. Night after night such meetings continued, often well into the early hours, as the college community experienced an unusual blessing and visitation from the Holy Spirit. Hundreds wept, prayed, confessed their sins and sought reconciliation with God and with each other, telling of release from sexual sins, substance abuse, resentment, anger, hatred and pride.[58]

In these verses we find a definition of the meaning of repentance, which is necessary in order to enjoy God's presence fully. Repentance is not easy. It involves turning away from sin: 'Let the wicked forsake his way and the evil man his thoughts' (v. 7a). A child once defined repentance as 'being sorry enough to stop'.

It also involves turning to God: 'Let him turn to the Lord, and he will have mercy on him, and to our God, for he will freely pardon' (v. 7b).

As Duncan Campbell writes, 'We may have succeeded in making people church-conscious, mission-conscious, or even crusade-conscious without making them God-conscious. The Church must recognise the basic fact that revival must ever be related to righteousness, and that the way to a revived Church is still the way of repentance and true holiness.'[59]

This is another of the distinguishing marks of the Holy Spirit in revival, according to Jonathan Edwards: 'If we see persons made sensible of the dreadful nature of sin, and of the displeasure of God against it; or their own miserable condition as they are in themselves by reason of sin and earnestly concerned for their eternal salvation, and sensible of their need of God, pity and help, and engaged to seek it in the use or the means that God has appointed, we may certainly conclude that it is from the Spirit of God.'[60]

The purpose of our return is to find mercy. The reassurance is that we will find pardon. No matter how far we have fallen, God will forgive us. Recently, I received a letter from a convicted murderer who has been on an Alpha course in a UK prison. He wrote:

Dear Nicky,
For a long time now I've searched for forgiveness for taking the life of an innocent person. From the age of five I've had beatings and sexual abuse from members of my family. When I realised what was happening I started running away and pinching to get money to help me get away. I robbed a friend's home which was supposed to be empty, was caught and panicked, and took a life.

For years I held bitter memories of my family and for the life I took I held sorrow. All my life I've searched for forgiveness. I've been in prison for 30 years. One night I went to church and they were speaking about Alpha . . .

He started going along to the course. After a few weeks he realised it was 'for real' and he started to enjoy the group talks. After one of the talks he gave his life to Christ and was filled with the Holy Spirit.

I held my eyes shut tight. After a couple of minutes a bright light came in from my right side and then disappeared. I felt so relaxed and at peace with my mind, the first time in 50 years.

I'm not good at putting words together but . . . after many many years I've found God, true Christianity and I've gone straight, no ducking and diving and I've learnt to trust in the Lord Jesus Christ.

Yours sincerely

Frank

PS. I've also learnt to forgive others who have hurt and sinned against me and it feels good being able to do this.

God forgives us on the basis of what the servant of the Lord has done for us (Is 53). His forgiveness is far greater than we could possibly imagine. How can this be? The prophet answers the question: '"For my thoughts are not your thoughts, neither are your ways my ways," declares the Lord. "As the heavens are higher than the earth, so are my ways higher than your ways and my thoughts than your thoughts"' (vv. 8–9). God's ways and thoughts are immeasurably higher than ours and there is an infinite gulf between him and us. We get some idea of this as we look at the 'work of his hands' in creation. More specifically, as we recognise the servant of the Lord, we realise how different he is from us. In him we see that God's plan of salvation is greater than we could ever imagine possible.

These verses are addressed first to those who do not think they need forgiveness. I remember someone on the Alpha course saying that he wanted to become a Christian. I explained to him that the first thing he needed to do was to repent. He said he could not think of anything in his life he needed to repent about. Even his wife confirmed that he was the nicest, kindest person one could ever imagine. Indeed, he is charming and delightful. Two years later, after becoming a Christian, he came forward for prayer at the end of a service. I asked him how he was, and I offered to pray with him. He said, 'I feel totally unworthy and sinful. I don't know how God could ever accept me or use me.' It was not that he had become a worse person over the two years. He had simply begun to see the difference between God's ways and thoughts and his own.

This passage also speaks to those who feel they are too bad to be forgiven. If God's forgiveness is higher and deeper than we could ever imagine, no one is too bad to be forgiven. God not only forgives, he wills to forget our sin, not through any pretence, but because sin has been completely dealt with on the cross. His forgiveness is also much greater than human forgiveness in that he goes on forgiving. As with the Prodigal Son, he gives us 'the best robe . . . a ring on [our] finger and sandals on [our] feet'. He brings the fattened calf, and says, 'Let's have a feast and celebrate' (Lk 15:22–23).

Velma Barfield led a tragic life of turmoil, anger, depression, violence and drug addiction. She poisoned four people, including her own mother, and ended up awaiting execution on Death Row. Shortly after her arrest, she turned to Christ and became a vibrant, committed Christian. She firmly believed that her sins had been completely forgiven by God. All that was left for her to do was to pay society's ultimate price. She did not take lightly the fact that she had committed horrific crimes. Nor did she take God's forgiveness lightly, for it had cost Christ his life on the cross. Yet through that death, she knew, God had demonstrated his love for sinners—even for a wretched sinner like herself. 'If I had the choice of living free on the outside [of prison] without my Lord, or living on Death Row with him,' she said repeatedly, 'I would choose Death Row.'

Just a few months before her last day, she finished writing her life story. She wrote, 'I want my story told because I hope it will help people understand what God can do in the life of one loathsome and desperate human being. I understand what the apostle [Paul] meant when he called himself the chief of sinners.'

A month after the execution, Billy Graham went into the North Carolina Correctional Institute for Women to take part in a special service. Virtually all the guards and inmates were present. He preached from John 3:16—'For God so loved the world that he gave his one and only Son, that whoever believes in him shall not perish but have eternal life'—pointing to the life of Velma Barfield as an example of what God can do in the life of a person who is committed to Christ. Prison, he told them, was one of the hardest places on earth to live a Christian life. One is under constant scrutiny, and many inmates are cynical about supposed religious conversions. But Velma had demonstrated the reality of Christ through her life, and everyone present at that service knew it. Of the people present, 200, including several guards, gave their lives to Christ.

While there, Billy also went to the cell where Velma had been held in maximum security before her execution. 'You know, since Velma's death, I just couldn't bring myself to come in here,' the warden told him. 'On the night of her execution, she was the happiest, most radiant human being I ever met.'[61]

When we come to God we will be astonished at the treasures he will lavish on us. For more than 2,000 years, tourists, grave robbers and, latterly, archaeologists had searched for the burial places of Egypt's Pharaohs. It was believed that nothing remained undisturbed, especially in the Royal Valley where the ancient monarchs had been buried for thousands of years. With only a few scraps of evidence, Howard Carter, the British archaeologist, carried on his dig using his own money because no one felt there was anything left to be discovered. He was convinced that one tomb remained. Twice during his six-year search he was within two metres of the first stone step leading to the burial chamber.

Finally, in 1922, Carter unlocked an ancient Egyptian tomb. 'Can you see anything?' his assistant asked as Carter's eyes adjusted to the semi-darkness. Carter could see well enough, but he had difficulty speaking because of the treasure spread out before him.

Nobody in the modern world had seen anything like it. The king's mummy lay within a nest of three coffins, the inner one of solid gold, the two outer ones of hammered gold covering wooden frames. On the king's head was a magnificent golden portrait mask, and numerous pieces of jewellery and amulets lay on the mummy and in its wrappings. The coffins and the stone sarcophagus were surrounded by four shrines of hammered gold over wood, covered with texts, which practically filled the burial chamber. Other rooms were crammed with furniture, statues, clothes, a chariot, weapons, staffs, chests, carved cobras, vases, daggers, jewels and a throne. It was, of course, the priceless tomb and treasure of King Tutankhamen (who reigned from 1352 to 1343 BC), the world's most exciting archaeological discovery.

Paul writes, 'No eye has seen, no ear has heard, no mind has conceived what God has prepared for those who love him' (1 Cor 2:9). The Holy Spirit gives us a foretaste in this life of what we will experience. Indeed, Paul describes the Holy Spirit as the down payment, our first instalment, of the wonderful inheritance to come.

The transforming power of God (vv. 10–13)

'As the rain and the snow come down from heaven, and do not return to it without watering the earth and making it

bud and flourish, so that it yields seed for the sower and bread for the eater, so is my word that goes out from my mouth: It will not return to me empty, but will accomplish what I desire and achieve the purpose for which I sent it. You will go out in joy and be led forth in peace; the mountains and hills will burst into song before you, and all the trees of the field will clap their hands. Instead of the thornbush will grow the pine tree, and instead of briers the myrtle will grow. This will be for the Lord's renown, for an everlasting sign, which will not be destroyed.'

God promises that our lives will be fruitful. 'As the rain and the snow come down from heaven, and do not return to it without watering the earth and making it bud and flourish, so that it yields seed for the sower and bread for the eater, so is my word that goes out from my mouth: It will not return to me empty, but will accomplish what I desire and achieve the purpose for which I sent it' (vv. 10–11).

We all recognise that there is an inevitability in nature. Gardening requires patience, but combine sun, seed, soil and moisture, and sooner or later there will be a crop. There is a similar law in the spiritual world. 'Plant' God's word, and in time you can be sure there will be fruit. To change the metaphor, it is good business to spread the word of God. The business will prosper. When God speaks, something always happens. Lives are changed, new seeds are planted, hungry souls are fed.

More than this, there will be an impact on the created world around us. 'You will go out in joy and be led forth in peace; the mountains and hills will burst into song before you, and all the trees of the field will clap their hands. Instead of the thornbush will grow the pine tree, and instead of briers the myrtle will grow. This will be for the Lord's renown, for an everlasting sign, which will not be destroyed' (vv. 12–13).

The immediate application of this passage was to the departure of the Jews from Babylon. Israel was to 'go out' from Babylon and back to Jerusalem in joy and peace. On their journey home nature itself would burst out with joy, exuberance and gladness. The mountains and hills, symbols of permanence, would burst into song and the trees would clap their hands.

This was partially fulfilled with the restoration of Israel under Ezra and Nehemiah, but the real return from exile began with the coming of Jesus: his life, death and resurrection on Easter morning. This climactic event is the springboard for the restoration and revival of the church as the kingdom of God continues to advance. However, the prophecy will not reach complete fulfilment until the return of Jesus Christ. Then, nature itself will be renewed and restored. Until that time, we wait in anticipation. As Paul writes, 'The creation waits in eager expectation for the sons of God to be revealed. For the creation was subjected to frustration, not by its own choice, but by the will of the one who subjected it, in hope that the creation itself will be liberated from its bondage to decay and brought into the glorious freedom of the children of God' (Rom 8:19–21).

God's liberating action in Jesus Christ does not merely concern us as human beings, it concerns his whole creation. The natural world is not simply some stage scenery for a drama in which the only actors are human beings. The created world itself is part of the drama. The Bible is not only the story of the human race, but the story of the whole of creation, although the human race plays a central and crucial role.

The created world is not a power in itself, as the Babylonians thought. God created the world as a home for the human race. He created the human family to be stewards of the whole of creation until the time comes for him to wrap up this world's history.

The first human family did not fulfil the calling for which they were created. They wanted to be not merely the stewards and the managers but the owners. The result was that not only were they alienated from God and one another but they were also alienated from nature. Nature itself became our enemy and now brings forth thorns and briers (Gen 3:17–18). This is a picture of all the difficulties of life: ill health, temptations, battles, worries and annoyances. They are the symbols of a distorted creation with its natural disasters, such as earthquakes and volcanoes.

The work of Jesus, as the 'last Adam', is to make right the wrongdoing of the first Adam (see 1 Corinthians 15:22, 45). Only in Jesus can God's purpose for the whole of his creation be fulfilled. We have his pledge in the resurrection of Jesus from the dead, and his guarantee in the giving of the Holy Spirit (2 Cor 5:1–5). We can believe that the whole created world is the work of God which is under his control and will eventually be brought to its true consummation because Jesus rose from the dead, conquering death and setting free the whole creation to be caught up in praise of its creator. The created world is, in Calvin's words, 'the theatre of his glory'. Adam failed and disobeyed, so God sent Jesus to be an example of true humanity. Through Jesus Christ we can be transformed, reflecting the glory of God as he planned from the beginning.

God's invitation has a very wide scope. He invites

all who hunger and thirst. No one is excluded because they do not have enough to offer. We need have no money. We need bring nothing with us. We must leave our sin behind us. God invites us to be part of this amazing plan. Of course we are free to refuse his invitation. But if we do we will tragically lose out. If, however, we respond by coming to God, he will satisfy the deepest longings of the human heart. He will show us his purpose for our lives and, as he pours out his love and generosity upon us, we will experience his transforming power. We shall have the joy of participating in his plans which will lead to a transformed earth reflecting the glory of God.

8

How Should Revival Affect Society?
Isaiah 58

In September 1995, Michael Cassidy, the leader of the Christian organisation African Enterprise, returned from a ten-day reconciliation mission to Rwanda. His team had found the nation in ruin and devastation. Rwanda is a nation of 6 million people with three distinct ethnic groups: the Hutu, who are primarily farmers, make up 90 per cent of the population; the Tutsi, who raise long-horn cattle; and the Twa, pygmoid people, who are chiefly potters and hunters. Although fifty years ago the East African revival began there, the history of the country has been one of see-saw revolutions and massacres. The bloody climax came in April 1994. First there was massive genocide on the part of the Hutu militia. This was followed by the revenge of the Tutsi Exile Liberation Army.

The African Enterprise team heard the latest figures: 1 million people dead, 2 million people implicated in the deaths, 250,000 widows, 450,000 orphans and over 1.5 million exiles. There were 48,000 prisoners awaiting trial. It would take forty years to process their trials by UK standards and

140–200 years by USA procedures, according to the Red Cross.

In trying to understand how a country which had experienced revival could also experience this cataclysm, and how some Christians could ever be involved in the genocide, Michael Cassidy pointed to two dangerous theologies: first, love of God without love of country and secondly, love of country without love of God. He then spoke of the danger of privatised religion, a religion which does not allow the Christian faith to penetrate the political, economic, social, business, professional and moral issues of the country. 'To worry an African about politics and economics had, alas, come to be thought of as unspiritual.'

Yet, in the Bible, love for God and love for our neighbour are inextricably linked. 'One of the unique features of the Biblical faith is that there is no genuine relation with God that is not at the same time a relation with the brother.'[62]

So the message of Isaiah 58, which probably describes the situation in Israel after the return from exile around 538 BC, is as important for us today as it was then. The prophet clearly believed it was a vital message: 'Shout it aloud, do not hold back. Raise your voice like a trumpet. Declare to my people their rebellion and to the house of Jacob their sins' (Is 58:1).

Love of God without love of our neighbour (vv. 1–5)

'Shout it aloud, do not hold back. Raise your voice like a trumpet. Declare to my people their rebellion and to the house of Jacob their sins. For day after day they seek me out; they seem eager to know my ways, as if they were a

nation that does what is right and has not forsaken the commands of its God. They ask me for just decisions and seem eager for God to come near them. "Why have we fasted," they say, "and you have not seen it? Why have we humbled ourselves, and you have not noticed?"

'Yet on the day of your fasting, you do as you please and exploit all your workers. Your fasting ends in quarrelling and strife, and in striking each other with wicked fists. You cannot fast as you do today and expect your voice to be heard on high. Is this the kind of fast I have chosen, only a day for a man to humble himself? Is it only for bowing one's head like a reed and for lying on sackcloth and ashes? Is that what you call a fast, a day acceptable to the Lord?'

God rebukes his people for their privatised religion. It is true that they were devoted and zealous in their religious practices (Is 58:2–3a). They prayed, fasted and humbled themselves. But the problem was that they did not obey the Lord in their treatment of others.

Although they fasted, they did not refrain from wrong behaviour. They were guilty of the exploitation of their workers (v. 3b). There was in-fighting, 'quarrelling and strife' (v. 4a) and violence: 'striking each other with wicked fists' (v. 4b). As so often in the church today, they were fighting one another rather than loving one another. It is so easy to get bogged down in our own little world and fail to see the bigger picture and the needs of the world around us. God rebuked the people because their confidence lay in words and ritual practices rather than in obedience, which would have resulted in a wide range of good works.

Love for our neighbour (vv. 6–12)

'Is not this the kind of fasting I have chosen: to loose the chains of injustice and untie the cords of the yoke, to set the oppressed free and break every yoke? Is it not to share your food with the hungry and to provide the poor wanderer with shelter—when you see the naked, to clothe him, and not to turn away from your own flesh and blood? Then your light will break forth like the dawn, and your healing will quickly appear; then your righteousness will go before you, and the glory of the Lord will be your rear guard. Then you will call, and the Lord will answer; you will cry for help, and he will say: Here am I.

'If you do away with the yoke of oppression, with the

*pointing finger and malicious talk, and if you spend your-
selves on behalf of the hungry and satisfy the needs of the
oppressed, then your light will rise in the darkness, and
your night will become like the noonday. The Lord will
guide you always; he will satisfy your needs in a sun-
scorched land and will strengthen your frame. You will
be like a well-watered garden, like a spring whose waters
never fail. Your people will rebuild the ancient ruins and
will raise up the age-old foundations; you will be called
Repairer of Broken Walls, Restorer of Streets with
Dwellings.'*

Neither fasting, nor any other kind of self-sacrificial
religious observance, is of any use unless it is geared
to the benefit of others and to the needs of society.

Of course, we do not love our neighbours if we withhold from them the good news of Jesus Christ. Yet evangelism and social action are partners, and both are needed in every local church programme as a responsible expression of Christian love. God equips the church to show this love by calling different people to different ministries and equipping them with appropriate gifts. Some are evangelists, some political activists and others are called to social service. For example, Billy Graham is called mainly to evangelism (although he contributes a great deal to social work by giving money generously for disaster relief and education). Others, like William Wilberforce and Martin Luther King, were called primarily to political activity, while Mother Teresa's primary calling was in the area of social service. God has given us the task of witnessing to Jesus through both speech and social action. Here the prophet concentrates on our social responsibilities.

Social action

In verse 6 he speaks of three scourges which need to be removed from society. First, there is injustice. Social action involves a quest for the creation of a just society. Secondly, he speaks about inhumanity—we must 'untie the cords of the yoke', that is, eliminate the ways in which people are treated like animals. Thirdly, he speaks about inequality—'set the oppressed free and break every yoke'. The removal of these causes of human need may involve political and economic activity in seeking to transform the structures of society.

South Africa is a clear example of a country where, until recently, all these three scourges were present. There was the appalling injustice of apartheid, which led, among other things, to imprisonment without trial and social segregation without reason. That seventy-seven black men found it necessary to leap to their deaths from the police station in Johannesburg was only one symptom of a manifestly unjust system.

Secondly, there was the inhumanity of the system. Nelson Mandela, in his autobiography, *Long Walk to Freedom*, describes the prison conditions on Robben Island. The lime quarry in which they were forced to work as slaves was the scene of fearful atrocities. Prisoners were beaten, abused and had dogs set on them. They were allowed no contact with the outside world. Initially, Mandela was allowed one letter every six months. Sometimes he would be told, 'Mandela, we have received a letter for you, but we cannot give it to you.' One letter from his wife was so heavily censored that not much more than the greeting was left. When he was caught reading a newspaper left behind by a guard, he was sentenced to three days in isolation on a starvation diet.

Thirdly, there was inequality. So pervasive was the apartheid system that blacks and whites were separated even in prison. The blacks were given less food and not allowed to wear long trousers. They were called 'boy' and treated like animals.

Part of the church in South Africa failed to act. Indeed, some even sought to uphold the system. However, others, like Archbishop Desmond Tutu and Michael Cassidy, did make a determined stand. Politically, Nelson Mandela led the fight. Some say Mandela is not a Christian. If so, his life stands as a rebuke to the church. However, the evidence suggests that he is a Christian. He wrote, 'I told them that I was a Christian and had always been a Christian.'[63] He taught a Bible class as a young man and regularly attended church on Robben Island. Certainly he demonstrated the fruit of the Spirit, especially in forgiving his enemies. He wrote, 'I knew that people expected me to harbour anger towards whites. But I had none . . . I wanted South Africa to see that I loved even my enemies while I hated the system that turned us against one another.'[64]

Mandela fought the system with courage and determination. Before being sentenced to prison he said,

> I know how gross is the discrimination, even behind the prison wall, against Africans . . . More powerful than my fear of the dreadful conditions to which I might be subjected in prison is my hatred for the dreadful conditions to which my people are subjected outside prison throughout this country . . . When my sentence has been completed . . . I will still be moved . . . to take up again, as best I can, the struggle for the removal of those injustices until they are finally abolished once and for all . . . [65]

Mandela refused to allow hatred for whites to enter his soul. On Robben Island he taught the young freedom fighters the same, lest they became like their captors. His concern was for all South Africans, regardless of their skin colour. After twenty-seven-and-a-half years in prison he was told he would be released during the next twenty-four hours, yet he asked for an extra week to allow him to say goodbye and to thank each of the prison staff. James Gregory, his jailer for twenty years, wrote a book called *Goodbye Bafana Nelson Mandela My Prisoner, My Friend*.[66] He and his family were guests of honour at the presidential inauguration. Indeed, throughout his imprisonment, Mandela was humane, dignified, unembittered, tolerant and forgiving. He has 'inspired a world prone to cynicism'.[67]

It is not always easy to recognise injustice, inhumanity and inequality. They abound around the world, but they also exist in our own society. One example is the issue of abortion. What could be more unjust than the killing of innocent babies before they are even born? What could be more inhumane than the way it is done? What could be more unequal than treating unborn children so differently from those who are slightly older? Christians need to be involved in the structures of our society at a local and national level in order to fight injustice, inhumanity and inequality wherever it is found.

Social service

The prophet now moves from social action, that is, the removal of the causes of human need, to social service, the direct relief of human need.

Verse 7 points to three areas of need. First, he points to the hungry—'Is it not to share your food with the hungry?' Millions of people die of starvation each year, even though God has provided enough for everyone's need. There is no political or economic reason that excuses the existence of food mountains while much of the world is starving. Thankfully there are those who are determined to change this situation.

In 1948 Bob Pierce, a young United States evangelist working under the auspices of Youth for Christ, went to China to make his first major Christian missions film, *China Challenge*. On Amoy (now Xiamen) Island in the Formosa Strait, at a school run by Christian missionaries for 400 Chinese girls, he encountered a ragged and hungry child named White Jade. Her father had beaten her for visiting the mission. The school, with not enough food for its pupils, had none to give her. Learning that the girl could be supported for US$25 a year, Dr Pierce gave the school's headmistress $5 he had in his pocket and promised to send more money.

In 1950, World Vision was formed as a new missionary service organisation with Pierce as president. World Vision set its course to care for the fatherless and widows, to help the poor and the starving, to care for the sick and to seek to present the gospel of Jesus Christ. In 1996 it helped over 5 million people in over 100 countries, through long-term community projects, focused especially on the needs of children, and emergency relief assisting people affected by conflict or disaster.

Another fine example is Bread for the World, an agency founded by Christians who believed they could best help the hungry, not by competing with World Vision, but by lobbying American Congress on behalf of the world's poor.

Secondly, the prophet points to homelessness—'to provide the poor wanderer with shelter'. There are people whose lands and homes have been appropriated in payment for debts. Millions worldwide still face a future robbed of hope by the lack of adequate shelter. In Calcutta alone 250,000 sleep in the streets at night. The problem of homelessness in Britain is obvious and well-documented.

Millard Fuller, a millionaire entrepreneur from Alabama, is someone who has responded to this call. He gave away his personal fortune and in 1976 founded an organisation on the simple premise that every human being deserves a decent place to live. Today, that organisation, Habitat for Humanity International, an ecumenical Christian housing ministry, organises hundreds of thousands of volunteers to build houses in over forty nations. It has built approximately 30,000 houses around the world, providing over 100,000 people with safe, decent, affordable shelter.

Thirdly, Isaiah points to poverty—'when you see the naked, to clothe him'. Lack of clothing is a sign of abject poverty. One fifth of the world is destitute and 800 million individuals are trapped in absolute poverty, a condition characterised by malnutrition, illiteracy, disease, squalid surroundings, high infant mortality and low life expectancy.

We hear statistics such as these and wonder how any individual can make the slightest bit of difference. But occasionally one does and this should inspire us. Bill Magee is a plastic surgeon who was shocked to find that in developing countries many children go through life with untreated cleft palates. They cannot smile, and their lips curl open in a constant sneer, making them the object of ridicule. Magee and his wife organised a programme called Operation Smile: planeloads of doctors and their assistants travel to Vietnam, the Philippines, Kenya, Russia and the Middle East in order to repair facial deformities. So far, they have operated on more than 36,000 children.

Dame Cicely Saunders is the founder of the modern hospice movement at St Christopher's Hospice in London. She was a social worker and nurse who was appalled at the way medical staff treated people who were dying. She believed that Christians would be able to offer the best combination of physical, emotional and spiritual care to those facing death. Having requalified as a doctor, she went on to establish a place where people could come to die with dignity and without pain. There are now 2,000 hospices in the United States alone.

The expression 'when you see' (v. 7b) is a telling one. Our first step is to have the eyes to see the need. Then we have a duty to act. Increasingly, we do see the world's needs through the media. Therefore, we have a responsibility to act. Often we shall be overwhelmed by the massive global scale of the problems and we shall wonder if we can really make a difference. One day a man was walking along a beach as the tide was receding. He saw tens of thousands of starfish stranded on the beach, drying out and slowly dying. He noticed a young boy picking up the starfish one at a time, and throwing them back into the sea. He approached the boy and said to him, 'With tens of thousands of those starfish lying up and down the beach you must feel like you're not making much of a difference.' As the boy tossed yet another starfish into the sea he turned to the man and said, 'I bet it made a difference to that one.'

Family life

The prophet adds an interesting practical observation: 'And not to turn away from your own flesh and blood' (v. 7b). It is possible to be socially sensitive but domestically negligent. The needs of our own family must be balanced with those of others. Indeed for many the family is the setting in which the love and compassion of God has to be exercised for the time being. For instance, since children need privacy and a safe environment, we must be careful about those we invite into our homes. Yet sadly some who care for the needs of others become so busy that they turn away from their own flesh and blood. Sometimes they neglect their own children or their own parents.

Occasionally, of course, it is not possible to meet the needs of our own family. There is a poignant section of Nelson Mandela's book when he speaks of 'a particularly beautiful tomato plant' he had grown in prison. He had 'coaxed it from a tender seedling to a robust plant that produced deep red fruit'. But then, either through some mistake or lack of care, the plant began to wither and decline, and he continued, 'Nothing I did would bring it back to health. When it finally died, I removed the roots from the soil, washed them and buried them in the corner of the garden.'[68] He then wrote to his wife, explaining what had happened. The incident brought to mind his feeling of inability to nourish many of the most important relationships in his life. When his mother died he was not allowed to go to the funeral. When his son was killed in a car crash, he was again refused permission. He describes how, after many years, he was able to touch his wife. 'I kissed and held my wife for the first time. It was a moment I had dreamed about a thousand times . . . It had been twenty-one years since I had even touched my wife's hand.'[69]

Those of us who are able to nurture our own families must do so. We are called to build strong family life, to care for our spouse, children and parents. In our desire to fulfil our wider social responsibilities we must not neglect to build a strong family life.

The results

Social action, social service and building family life are not tiresome burdens but a joy. The prophet now presents the people with an astonishing array of promises which follow obedience to God's commands. First, God promises a new beginning: 'Then your light will break forth like the dawn' (v. 8a). Secondly, he promises restoration and healing: 'Your healing will quickly appear' (vv. 8–9). Literally, the word for healing means the new layer of skin that grows over a wound that is healing.[70] Thirdly, God promises security and protection: 'Then your righteousness will go before you, and the glory of the Lord will be your rear guard' (v. 8b). Fourthly, we can expect answered prayer: 'Then you will call, and the Lord will answer; you will cry for help, and he will say: Here am I' (v. 9a).

Here, Isaiah interrupts the flow of promises with a further summary of the conditions. He repeats the need to do away with the yoke of oppression and for people to spend themselves 'on behalf of the hungry and satisfy the needs of the oppressed' (v. 10a). But he adds that it is also necessary to 'do away . . . with the pointing finger and malicious talk' (v. 9b). An advanced social conscience and a flourishing ministry can be marred by a critical attitude along with half-truths, gossip and slander.

In the following verse God continues the array of

promises. He promises to bring light in the darkness: 5
'then your light will rise in the darkness, and your
night will become like the noonday' (v. 10b). Sixthly,
he promises guidance: 'The Lord will guide you
always; he will satisfy your needs in a sun-scorched
land' (v. 11a). Seventhly, he promises strength: 'and
will strengthen your frame' (v. 11a). Literally, this
means that your bones will be made young again.
'Bones' signify the whole person made strong and
equipped for fighting.

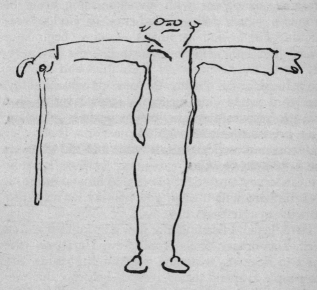

Eighthly, he promises fresh resources from within:
'You will be like a well-watered garden, like a spring
whose waters never fail' (v. 11b). Ninthly, rebuilding:
'Your people will rebuild the ancient ruins and will
raise up the age-old foundations; you will be called
Repairer of Broken Walls, Restorer of Streets with

Dwellings' (v. 12). This is similar to the promise in Isaiah 61:4.

Love of God combined with love of our neighbour (vv. 13–14)

'If you keep your feet from breaking the Sabbath and from doing as you please on my holy day, if you call the Sabbath a delight and the Lord's holy day honourable, and if you honour it by not going your own way and not doing as you please or speaking idle words, then you will find your joy in the Lord, and I will cause you to ride on the heights of the land and to feast on the inheritance of your father Jacob.' The mouth of the Lord has spoken.

At the end of the chapter the prophet returns to the theme of loving God. Love of God without love of our neighbour is not enough. But neither is love of our neighbour without love of God.

The call to keep the Sabbath is a call to consecrate life's timetable to God. It means to have a heart so captivated by God that to set aside time with him is an 'exquisite delight'. The Sabbath was a symbol of a whole life and heart devoted and submitted to the Lord. The key phrase is 'not doing as you please' (v. 13b). This echoes verse 3b where the problem with their fasting was that they continued to do as they pleased.

If we love the Lord above all else, we will want to do his pleasure rather than our own. As we combine our love for our neighbour with a love for God he promises us three things. First, joy: we will 'find [our] joy in the Lord' (v. 14a). Secondly he promises that we will 'ride on the heights' (v. 14a). This speaks of confidence in the face of life's problems, a capacity to ride high over oppression and obstacles, much as a plane does when it encounters turbulence and needs to fly higher. Thirdly, we will find satisfaction. We will 'feast', enjoying all the covenant blessings and the undisturbed possession of the land. These blessings are guaranteed because 'the mouth of the Lord has spoken' (v. 14b).

We need to get both our 'vertical' relationship with God and our 'horizontal' relationships with others right. Jesus exemplified this. The vertical and the horizontal met at the cross as Jesus looked up to his Father and stretched out his arms to the world.

True revival must have this combination, as did the eighteenth-century revival in Britain. George White-field always remembered the needs of the poor and used to 'nourish [his] acquaintances with the rich for the benefit of the poor'. Indeed, he was accused of being a spiritual pick-pocket! John Wesley was not only a preacher, he was also a prophet of social right-eousness. He was the author of a book on the slave trade, in which he totally denounced this inhuman traffic, when it was unthinkingly accepted by the vast majority of his contemporaries. At a time of growing wealth and empire, eventual victory over Napoleon and the beginnings of the industrial revolution, the revival fuelled a sense of hope and brought about social change. Literacy increased among the under-privileged, prisons were reformed (especially through the work of John Howard, a friend of Wesley's), and many who had been touched by revival gave them-selves to all kinds of social action. Historian K. S. Latourette concludes that although the climate of the time in Europe was anti-faith, 'life was breaking out again in Christianity' and that those who were part of it 'were to shape much of mankind'.[71]

The major legislative social gains of the nineteenth century were achieved against the background of powerful spiritual movements. The historian Arnold Toynbee was of the clear opinion that the eighteenth-century evangelical revival saved Britain from the revolutionary experience that ravaged the continent of Europe, particularly France, at that time. Revival gave the British nation a social conscience, producing people who campaigned for the abolition of slavery and bringing women and children up from the mines and boys down from the chimneys. Revival contributed also to a greater concern for prisoners and the insane, a reduction in hours of work and a care for the living conditions of the poor.

As we have seen, the Welsh revival of 1904–5 brought lasting changes to the community. One example is the decrease of drunkenness and related crimes. The following figures for the total convictions for drunkenness in Glamorgan were released by the Chief Constable of Cardiff four years after the outbreak of the revival:

1902	9,298
1903	10,528
1904	11,282
1905	8,164
1906	5,490
1907	5,615

Drunkenness is often the spur to many other crimes, such as child abuse and wife battering. The Chief Constable said, 'The decrease in drunkenness has undoubtedly been most marked where the Revivalists have had the largest following. People started to repay shopkeepers who had written the debts off as bad debts. Women who sued one another in the courts prayed side by side at the same meeting.' Illegitimate births declined. Stolen goods were returned and, in several places, magistrates were presented with white gloves, signifying that there were no cases left to try.

Sectarianism and suspicion also ended. 'Denominational walls, as high perhaps in Wales as in most countries, fell down as did Jericho's walls.'[72] Edwin Orr, one of the greatest authorities on the history of revivals, wrote, 'Revival united the denominations as one body, filled the chapels nightly, renewed family ties, changed lives in mines and factories, often crowded streets with huge processions, abated the social vices and diminished crime.'

True and lasting revival changes not only human hearts, but also communities and institutions. Love for God and love for neighbour go hand in hand. Bishop Lesslie Newbigin, speaking from his considerable experience writes:

Christian programmes for justice and compassion . . . severed from their proper roots in the local liturgical and sacramental life of the congregation . . . lose their character as signs of the presence of Christ and risk becoming mere crusades fuelled by a moralism that can become self-righteous. And the life of the worshipping congregation, severed from its proper expression in compassionate service to the secular community around it, risks becoming a self-centred existence serving only the needs and desires of its members.[73]

We must not sit around waiting for revival to happen. We are called to respond to God's love for us, to show our love for God by loving our neighbour. This means communicating the message of the gospel. It involves attacking the causes of human need by social action, and the direct relief of human need by social service.

Charles Grandison Finney (1792–1875), an American lawyer and one of history's greatest evangelists, is considered by many to be the forerunner of modern evangelism. He wrote:

> The great business of the church is to reform the world—to put away every kind of sin. The Christian church was designed to make aggressive movements in every direction, to lift her voice and put forth her energies against iniquity in high and low places, to reform individuals, communities and governments, until every form of iniquity is driven from the earth.[74]

9

What Is the Source of Revival?
Isaiah 61:1–11

In 1972 my spiritual life was in a mess, to put it mildly
. . . Perhaps I had spent too long in theological education, I don't know, but whatever the reason I knew
that my spiritual life was at a crisis point. My heart
hadn't kept pace with my head. Sometimes when I
was teaching New Testament theology, I found myself
thinking: 'You hypocrite. You don't really believe this,
do you?' But I was trapped. I had to go along with the
show. I couldn't let the side down. I had to pretend all
was well.

The feeling of spiritual emptiness, or disenchantment,
was especially acute when I gave a series of lectures on
the Holy Spirit . . . All I was sure of was my spiritual
void.

In myself I was fairly normal. I wasn't a psychiatric
mess, a quivering bundle of nerves or anything like that.
I was thirty-seven at the time, a normal, balanced,
healthy person with no experience of clinical or patholo-
gical depression. I was happily married . . . we were
blessed with four delightful children. But the experience
of Christianity had somehow disappeared from my life.
The great truths . . . had lost their fire and their power to
convince. To all intents and purposes I was all right, but I
knew that if God did not intervene soon my whole Christian existence was finished. It was that desperate. . . .

To make matters worse, I was faced with a growing number of young [people] at college whose assurance, ebullience and Christ-filled lives mocked my impoverished spirit. [Eventually, one Sunday evening,] I found myself on my knees saying, 'Lord, you know the mess I am in right now. And yet I owe you so much . . . I thank you that you called me into Christian ministry and empowered me for your service. But Lord, I have become so busy in your service that I have lost you somehow. I have been so self-centred and interested in doing what I want that I have forced you out of my life. I cannot live a hypocritical life any more. Unless you fill me again with your Spirit, I cannot go on! . . . God spoke to me in a still small voice . . . Christ came again into my longing life and claimed me as his own.

There was only one unusual thing: a distinct word came echoing into my mind over and over again: *Shamayim, Shamayim!* What did it mean? Later it was to dawn on me—of course! *Shamayim* is the Hebrew word for heaven. And that evening was a foretaste of heaven, a lovely knowledge that in a simple way I had encountered the Spirit in a real way and I was home again.

What difference did it make? A great deal. It restored me to a great love of Christ, a deep desire to read the Scriptures, a longing to share the Christian faith with others and a desire to praise God. I was later to learn that these are characteristics of the work of the Holy Spirit . . . Without that experience of the Spirit I am sure that the story of St Nic's [his first parish as vicar] would not have happened in the way it did . . . I would never have had the spiritual resources to lead the congregation, neither would I have had insight and vision to see God at work in the fellowship. God had to make me usable.

These are the words of Dr George Carey, Archbishop of Canterbury.[75]

On one occasion, Jesus was invited to preach before his family and friends. The local Rabbi asked him to read the lesson and speak afterwards. He stood up and began to read Isaiah 61:1–3 from the scroll which had been given to him: 'The Spirit of the Sovereign Lord is on me, because the Lord has anointed me to preach good news to the poor. He has sent me to bind up the broken-hearted, to proclaim freedom for the captives and release from darkness for the prisoners, to proclaim the year of the Lord's favour.' At the end, he handed back the scroll, and sat down. Then he began his talk with these words, 'Today this scripture is fulfilled in your hearing' (Lk 4:21). The people said, 'Who is this? Isn't this Joseph's son?' At first they were very excited, but as he made it clear that the Gentiles also might be shown God's favour, they became furious. They seized him and dragged him to a precipice, in order to throw him off it, but somehow he walked through their midst and went on his way.

With much Old Testament prophecy, we can see three levels of fulfilment. As with a landscape, there is a foreground, a middle ground and a background. The foreground is the more immediate context; the middle ground is often hundreds of years ahead (in this case, the coming of Jesus); the background may be even further ahead, such as fulfilment of this prophecy in the church, or the second coming of Jesus.

The historical setting for Isaiah 61:1–11 is probably the era just after the exile. In 539 BC Cyrus, King of Persia, defeated the Babylonian army and entered Babylon. In 538 he issued an edict concerning the rebuilding of the temple of Jerusalem. He allowed Jews to return home to Babylon and begin rebuilding. He gave back the temple vessels carried off when the city was captured (Ezra 6:3 and following). In 537 BC a small number of Israelites returned. The prophetic words in Isaiah 61 address a weary and disheartened people facing a massive task of rebuilding a few years later.

As we have seen, the second level and, indeed, the supreme fulfilment is in Jesus. The third level is the events on the Day of Pentecost, when Jesus sent his Spirit to the church. God has anointed all Christians with the same Spirit that anointed Jesus: in the same way and for the same purposes we see described in these verses. This third level of fulfilment makes the passage relevant to those in church history and to all of us today. This application is our main concern in this chapter. However, it is important to bear in mind that the passage also had both an immediate historical fulfilment and, in Jesus, a central fulfilment.

The practice of 'anointing' (v.1) in the Old Testament was reserved mainly for kings, and also for priests. It was not usual for prophets to be anointed, Elisha being an exception (1 Kings 19:16). Anointing was often connected with the impartation of the Holy Spirit (see 1 Samuel 16:13; 2 Samuel 23:1–7). In this passage of Isaiah, we see three results of the anointing of the Holy Spirit which help us understand why we need such an anointing today.

We have power to restore the lives of individuals (vv. 1–3)

The Spirit of the Sovereign Lord is on me, because the Lord has anointed me to preach good news to the poor. He has sent me to bind up the broken-hearted, to proclaim freedom for the captives and release from darkness for the prisoners, to proclaim the year of the Lord's favour and the day of vengeance of our God, to comfort all who mourn, and provide for those who grieve in Zion—to bestow on them a crown of beauty instead of ashes, the oil of gladness instead of mourning, and a garment of praise instead of a spirit of despair. They will be called oaks of righteousness, a planting of the Lord for the display of his splendour.

The American church leader, John Wimber, has defined ministry as 'meeting the needs of others with the resources of God'. The anointing of the Spirit gives us power and authority to do exactly that.

First, we are enabled to speak God's word, 'to preach good news to the poor' (v. 1). The Greek word for 'to preach the good news' is *euangelizomai*,[76] from which we get the word 'evangelise'. The 'poor' are the downtrodden, the socially and materially disadvantaged and those burdened by guilt. We are given authority to tell them that all can receive hope, be forgiven, and that their guilt can be removed. The Spirit of God anoints and equips us to speak the word of God with boldness and power.

Evan Roberts, the man at the centre of the Welsh revival of 1904–5, told how the Spirit of God gave him an overwhelming experience of God's love. He was filled with compassion and wrote, 'I felt ablaze with a desire to go through the length and breadth of Wales to tell of the Saviour: and had it been possible, I was willing to pay God for doing so.'[77]

Secondly, the Spirit of God brings healing. We are anointed 'to bind up the broken-hearted' (v. 1). The word for 'bind up' means to bandage, soothe, heal and to restore to wholeness. 'Broken-hearted' covers any and every human breakdown: physical, emotional and spiritual. We have a God-given authority to bring healing to the broken hearts, lives and relationships around us.

Our society is in desperate need of this ministry. In a recent *Sunday Times* article about rock music, entitled, 'Everybody hurts sometimes', the journalist wrote, 'Rock has always had its gloomier side, but recently the anguish and depression have taken a turn for the worse.' He reported, 'The Samaritans are right to place their full-page ads in the music press.' He quoted a letter from a reader:

> Welcome to the afterlife. This is our hell, our souls are tortured before we depart this horrible, uncomprehending, self-interested planet. Why don't we kill ourselves? . . . Is it worth facing 50 more years of this horror? The horror of waking up every morning wanting to die? No! Do what makes you happy.

He said, 'Most of the correspondence is about desperately trying to battle with depression . . .'[78]

However, it is not just the rock music world, but this whole generation, that is so often broken-hearted and in need of healing.

Thirdly, we are able to proclaim deliverance. We are anointed 'to proclaim freedom for the captives and release from darkness for the prisoners, to proclaim the year of the Lord's favour and the day of vengeance of our God' (v. 2). The 'year of the Lord's favour' probably means the Jubilee year. The people of Israel were meant to celebrate the Jubilee year every fifty years (although they may not have done so). The trumpet was to sound and they were to proclaim liberty throughout the land and to all its inhabitants. Everyone was to return to his family property and to his own clan. The slaves and hired workers and their children were to be released to go back to their own clans. The year of Jubilee was a time when freedom was proclaimed for the captives and release for the prisoners (see Leviticus 25:8–55).

Although Cyrus had in effect brought freedom for the Jews to return from exile, only a few actually returned. They did not seem to appreciate their freedom. Similarly, when the slaves in the USA were set free, many did not believe it. Their former owners had to tell them, 'You are free.' Many Christians today would say that Jesus sets people free, but they have not experienced that freedom themselves. Jesus said, 'If the Son sets you free, you will be free indeed' (Jn 8:36). He frees us from habitual sin, addictions, and the burdens of hatred and rejection. We have been given 'the glorious freedom of the children of God' (Rom 8:21). As Christians, we often fail to appreciate that we have the authority of God to proclaim this freedom to one another.

When Jesus read from Isaiah at the synagogue in Nazareth (Lk 4:18–19), he stopped his reading at this point and sat down. He did not go on to speak of the 'day of vengeance of our God'. The people listening in Nazareth would have taken this verse to apply to God's vengeance on those outside Israel. Jesus in fact went on to speak about God's favour extending to those outside Israel. Jesus' first coming was not about vengeance, but salvation and grace. He said, 'For God did not send his Son into the world to condemn the world, but to save the world through him' (Jn 3:17). When he comes again there will be a 'day' of judgement, which may be contrasted with the current 'year' of favour: we need to make the most of our present opportunity to proclaim God's grace.

Fourthly, we are given authority 'to comfort all who mourn, and provide for those who grieve in Zion—to bestow on them a crown of beauty instead of ashes, the oil of gladness instead of mourning, and a garment of praise instead of a spirit of despair' (vv. 2–3). The word 'mourn' occurs frequently in reference to grieving for the dead, but covers all the sadnesses of life. Those who 'grieve' are the downcast and depressed. We are given authority to lift them into God's presence. To 'bestow' means to put, place, assign or appoint. To bestow 'beauty' for 'ashes' is an exact and complete substitution. Oil was used to make the face shine when otherwise it would look sad, and was associated with a time of gladness (Ps 23:5; 45:7). 'Garments of praise' suggests an array of new life expressed in spontaneous praise.

The result of these ministries (preaching good news, healing, delivering and comforting) is seen in the second half of verse 3: 'They will be called oaks of righteousness, a planting of the Lord for the display of his splendour' (v. 3). People who were previously impoverished, imprisoned and embittered are now enriched, free and joyful: a new life has been planted. More than that, they now have a new maturity, and are able to be a source of strength to others. The transformation in their lives is a visible testimony to the working of God's Spirit.

I recently received a brochure from the International Tree Foundation headed 'Trees are Life'. The description of trees struck me as a wonderful picture of the life-giving ministry of the Spirit. It says:

Trees are truly life-giving, providing food and shelter for man and beast from sun, wind and rain. Trees help maintain the water table and regulate rainfall in the tropics. They filter the air, and convert carbon dioxide to oxygen. They house and feed birds, animals and insects; they enrich and retain the soil; support fungi; and are a rich source of medicines. They provide timber for buildings, furniture and paper and still, sadly, fuel for warmth and cooking. Literally holding the earth together with their root networks, they prevent the creation of deserts and dustbowls. All this, and a thing of beauty . . . .[79]

Trees transform everything around them. So do 'oaks of righteousness'.

The long-term effect of the ministry of the Holy Spirit is not just to give us the authority to bless the people around us and see their lives turned around; it is to put them back on their feet and to empower them, in turn, to support others who are in need.

Billy Graham gave his life to Christ as a shy and timid sixteen-year-old. When he first tried preaching he learned four forty-five-minute sermons by heart, but he was so nervous he galloped through them in about eight minutes. He practised preaching in the

still neither useful nor beautiful Cecil.

woods to squirrels and rabbits, but churches would not have him. His passion—not to be a preacher but to tell others about Christ—was still strong. Then, one day, an opportunity arose to preach to a hundred people. He gave an invitation and thirty-two people came forward.

In 1946, Billy Graham heard Stephen Olford speak at Hildenborough Hall in England on the subject 'Be not drunk with wine—but be filled with the Spirit' (Eph 5:18). Billy Graham said that he could sense that 'Stephen had something in his life I wanted to capture—he had a dynamic, a thrill, an exhilaration about him'. They arranged to meet together for two days in a hotel in Pontypridd, Wales. Olford expounded 'the fullness of the Holy Spirit in the life of the believer', recalling: 'I gave him my testimony of how God completely turned my life inside out—an experience of the Holy Spirit in his fullness and anointing. As I talked, and I can see him now, those marvellous eyes glistening with tears, he said, "Stephen, I see it, that's what I want. That's what I need in my life."' They knelt down and prayed together. Finally, Billy Graham said, 'My heart is so flooded with the Holy Spirit.' They went from praying to praising. 'We were laughing and praising God. Billy Graham walked back and forth across the room, crying out, "I'm filled! This is the turning point in my life. This will revolutionise my ministry."' That evening, Olford recalls, 'As Billy rose to speak, he was a man absolutely anointed.'

In 1949 Graham led a crusade in Los Angeles. For three weeks he preached in a tent which held 6,100 people. Then, not knowing whether to continue, he asked God for a sign. At 2am the phone rang. It was Stuart Hamblen, a Texan cowboy in his late thirties and a well known radio host on the West Coast. He had a daily radio programme, was a great hunter, a successful race-horse owner, a gambler and a heavy drinker. He went to see Graham that night and, after much personal struggle, gave his life to Christ. The resulting publicity was enormous and hundreds of newcomers flocked to the big tent. Jim Vaus, a notorious criminal, heard Hamblen talking about the crusade on the radio, and decided to go and hear Graham out of curiosity. He was converted and the news spread throughout America. The tent had to be enlarged and Billy Graham continued the crusade for several more weeks. On the last night more than 9,000 squeezed into the tent: the largest audience of its kind for thirty years.

In 1954 Billy Graham signed a three-month contract to hire the 12,000-seater Harringay Arena in North London. The stadium owner later admitted that he expected the contract to be broken within two weeks, as no speaker had ever filled it for more than one night. The press were hostile. One headline was, 'Silly Billy'. The crusade was due to start on 1st March. That evening, despite bad weather, the stadium was packed, with thousands more outside. Billy Graham preached from John 3:16: 'For God so loved the world that he gave his one and only Son, that whoever believes in him shall not perish but have eternal life.' Except the second night, when there was snow and rain, Harringay Arena was full every night for three months.

Billy Graham had released Britons from their reticence; it suddenly became easy to talk about religion. Tongue-tied English Christians had the best opportunity of their lives, and clergyman visiting in their parishes found that small talk vanished quickly. Billy

Graham was the topic of conversation in homes, factories, clubs and pubs. Even more extraordinary was the transformation of the London Underground. 'From the seemingly endless queues waiting at the station for tickets, one hears wave after wave of song rolling back towards the street,' ran a letter in *The Daily Telegraph*. 'The tube trains are packed with these singing multitudes and there is a smile on every face. This quite spontaneous demonstration of Christian joy is most impressive and one cannot fail to observe the effect it has on passengers who board the trains at subsequent stations.'

The press turned from criticism to admiration and support. On Good Friday 40,000 were present at a Hyde Park rally covering half a square mile. Two jet aircraft passed overhead forming a cross in their vapour trail as Graham spoke. He quoted, 'God forbid that I should boast, save in the cross of our Lord Jesus Christ.' At the closing service, held at Wembley on 22nd May 1954, 120,000 people including the Archbishop of Canterbury, the Lord Mayor of London, and several MPs listened to Graham's address: 'Choose this day whom you will serve.' Some 2,000 people waded through the mud to respond to the invitation. Geoffrey Fisher, the Archbishop of Canterbury, pronounced the benediction, and the people sang 'To God Be the Glory'. As he left the platform, the Archbishop told Grady Wilson, Billy Graham's close friend and assistant, 'We may never again see a sight like that this side of heaven.' Grady was so moved that he forgot protocol and threw his arm around Dr Fisher. 'That's right, Brother Archbishop!' he agreed enthusiastically.

England was on the brink of revival and Graham said later that he always regretted not staying longer.

When he returned to London for a crusade at Earls Court in 1966, he had fifty-two Anglican clergymen sitting on the platform one night, all of whom had been converted in the Harringay meetings twelve years before.

Billy Graham has now preached to over 200 million people in person about Jesus Christ. He has been the trusted friend and confidant of nine US presidents. In December 1996 half of the world's population, 2.5 billion people, had the opportunity to see or hear him on television or radio.

But Billy Graham does not like statistics. He says, 'How can you put a reconciled home, a transformed drunkard, or a new selfless attitude into cold statistics?' He added, 'You have no idea how sick I get of the name Billy Graham and how wonderful and thrilling the name of Christ sounds in my ears.'

One USA governor said, 'He is a brilliant spark, full of drive, zeal and dedication who inspires others to their best efforts. He walks with an even step among the humble and moves with towering stature with the mighty.' Like Evan Roberts and many others before him Billy Graham is a man anointed by the Spirit of God.[80]

We have power to rebuild the community of the people of God (vv. 4–9)

They will rebuild the ancient ruins and restore the places long devastated; they will renew the ruined cities that have been devastated for generations. Aliens will shepherd your flocks; foreigners will work your fields and vineyards. And you will be called priests of the Lord, you will be named ministers of our God. You will feed on the wealth of nations, and in their riches you will boast.

Instead of their shame my people will receive a double portion, and instead of disgrace they will rejoice in their inheritance; and so they will inherit a double portion in their land, and everlasting joy will be theirs.

'For I, the Lord, love justice; I hate robbery and iniquity. In my faithfulness I will reward them and make an ever-lasting covenant with them. Their descendants will be known among the nations and their offspring among the peoples. All who see them will acknowledge that they are a people the Lord has blessed.'

The work of the Holy Spirit has a knock-on effect. The circles of blessing never cease to spread. First, the prophet is empowered. Through him, broken people are restored. They in turn, given their new strength, are able to rebuild their country. This even inspires the surrounding nations to co-operate with what God is doing. The Jews will be regarded as priests and ministers (v. 6) which foreshadows the idea of the priesthood of all believers in the New Testament (1 Pet 2:9). The people of Israel would be enriched by their former plunderers. Christians today may receive material and financial support from unexpected sources (v. 6).

William Booth, founder of the Salvation Army, was once offered £100 by the Marquis of Queensberry, a well-known agnostic. A Christian gentleman advised Booth 'not to take the infidel's dirty money'. General Booth replied, 'My only regret about the matter is that it was not £1,000, and if the money is dirty, we will wash it in the tears of the widows and orphans.' A similar incident occurred on board a ship, where some betting had taken place. 'An old gambler had gained the sum of £27 10s. The General said to the man, "The best use you can make of that money is to hand it over to me for the Salvation Army." "Well," replied the man, quite taken aback by the proposal, "I don't mind if I do," and placed the money in General Booth's hands.'[81]

God promises that instead of their shame the people of Israel will receive a double portion of God's blessing (v. 7). This contrasts with the double portion they received for their sins, the great misery of their captivity. Now God's people will inherit 'a double portion' of heavenly joys, just as Job, after intense suffering, received at the end of his life twice as much as he had had before. God will remember his covenant with his people (vv. 8–9). The Lord's people will be totally transformed. They will be distinct, unique, quite different from other people. And everyone will know that this is because God has blessed them.

Sadly, disunity can often undermine this perception. Unity in the church is part of rebuilding the community of God's people. When the church is united then 'all who see them will acknowledge that they are a people that the Lord has blessed' (v. 9). Jesus prayed for all those who would believe in him 'that all of them may be one . . . so that the world may believe' (Jn 17:20–21). Unity was a distinctive feature of the early church (see, for example, Acts 1–4) and is an important precursor to and factor in revival.

In the 1858 New York revival, thousands of Christians of many different denominations regularly met together to pray for God's blessing on the church and their nation. This united action amazed unbelievers and led the author Samuel Prime, an eyewitness to the revival, to write, 'Christians of both sexes, of all ages, of different denominations came together on one common platform of brotherhood in Christ.'

And he added, 'The great truth established by this revival is the cardinal doctrine of Christian union; oneness of the church; a real unity; a oneness of all her members in Christ, the head.'[82]

Paul writes of 'the unity of the Spirit' (Eph 4:3). The Holy Spirit alone can bring about genuine unity in the church. Raniero Cantalamessa wrote of his experience of being filled with the Holy Spirit. He received a vision of the cross of Christ, and was convinced at that moment that this renewal goes straight to the heart of the gospel, which is the cross of Jesus Christ. Of the effect the experience had on his life, he wrote, 'The Scriptures came alive'—he saw the Bible in a new light, as 'the passionate word of a father to his children'. He also had a new desire for prayer, for 'deep-down communication'.

Since then Raniero Cantalamessa has had a remarkable ministry, not only as a preacher, but also as an ambassador for reconciliation and unity. I remember hearing him at a conference in 1991, where he spoke about how the unity of the Spirit precedes institutional unity. He pointed to Acts 10, where Peter saw that the Holy Spirit had come upon the Gentiles, and said, 'They have received the Holy Spirit just as we have' (v. 47). Later, Peter went on to say, 'So if God gave them the same gift as he gave us, who believed in the Lord Jesus Christ, who was I to think that I could oppose God?' (Acts 11:17). Raniero Cantalamessa commented, 'With our own eyes we have seen the same miracle on a world-wide scale. What unites us is infinitely greater than what divides us. He quoted Tertullian: 'Pagans say of Christians, "See how they love one another."' He also quoted St John of the Cross: 'When love is lacking, sow love and you will soon gather love.' 'When Christians quarrel,'

Cantalamessa said, 'they say to God, "Choose between us and them." But the Father loves all his children. We should say, "We accept as our brothers all whom you receive as your children."'

However, unity should not be sought at the expense of truth. Right and wrong matter to God. God says, 'For I, the Lord, love justice; I hate robbery and iniquity' (v. 8). We have already looked at four of the five marks of the Spirit of God expounded by Jonathan Edwards in his treatise on revival. The fifth one is when the Spirit 'operates as a spirit of truth, leading persons to truth, convincing them of those things that are true, we may safely determine that it is a right and true spirit'.[83]

Truth is to be found in a Person. Jesus said, 'I am the truth' (Jn 14:6). It is around him that we unite. As Cantalamessa put it, 'Jesus Christ is the only heritage we share undivided.' In him alone are unity and truth. When people in the church unite around the essential truth of the Christian faith then all who see them will acknowledge that they are people the Lord has blessed (v. 9). The unity of the people of God is one of the surest fruits of the Holy Spirit.

We have power to affect the entire community (vv. 10–11)

I delight greatly in the Lord; my soul rejoices in my God. For he has clothed me with garments of salvation and arrayed me in a robe of righteousness, as a bridegroom adorns his head like a priest, and as a bride adorns herself with her jewels. For as the soil makes the young plant come up and a garden causes seeds to grow, so the Sovereign Lord will make righteousness and praise spring up before all nations.

At the end of the chapter the prophet speaks again. He is full of joy: 'I delight greatly in the Lord; my soul rejoices in my God. For he has clothed me with garments of salvation and arrayed me in a robe of righteousness, as a bridegroom adorns his head like a priest, and as a bride adorns herself with her jewels' (v. 10). The 'robe of righteousness' suggests something festive and wholly undeserved. This is the kind of righteousness that Paul speaks of in the New Testament. 'This righteousness from God comes through faith in Jesus Christ to all who believe. There is no difference, for all have sinned and fall short of the glory of God, and are justified freely by his grace through the redemption that came by Christ Jesus' (Rom 3:22–23). Isaiah's picture of a wedding is one of a bride and bridegroom who are both as attractive as they can be for their great day.

Isaiah moves from a picture of a wedding to a picture of a garden: 'For as the soil makes the young plant come up and a garden causes seeds to grow, so the Sovereign Lord will make righteousness and praise spring up before all nations' (v. 11). What happens to the people of God will affect all the nations. Indeed, the work of the revived church is to bring the nations to God, so that they, too, praise him.

George Whitefield (1714–1770) was the outstanding preacher of the Great Awakening in the eighteenth century. He recorded in his journal how he 'was filled with the Holy Ghost. Oh, that all who deny the promise of the Father, might thus receive it themselves! Oh, that all were partakers of my joy!'[84]

He also describes how on one occasion

he began to pray a brief prayer before addressing the assembly but to his own astonishment could not stop.

Petitions, praises, raptures poured forth from his lips: 'A wonderful power was in that room' . . . Whitefield's prayer was drowned by cries which, he was sure, could be heard a great way off . . . . Cries and groans and quaking had sometimes accompanied the preaching . . . 'thousands cried out so that they almost drowned my voice'. Whitefield did not doubt this time that the Spirit of God was present in fire and love and force. Men and women dropped as dead, then revived, then fainted again as Whitefield preached on, swept up into the contemplation of Christ's 'all-constraining, free and everlasting love' until, as he reached the last appeal to come to the Cross and receive the grace of God, Whitefield himself fell into a swoon. For a few moments the Tennent brothers believed he was dead. He revived, mounted his horse with their help, and together the three men travelled no less than twenty miles home through the woods by moonlight, singing as they rode.[85]

As we have seen, even secular historians agree that it was the revival that occurred at the time of Whitefield and Wesley that probably saved England from an experience such as the French Revolution.

Charles Finney described his experience of the Holy Spirit which occurred in 1821:

The Holy Spirit descended upon me in a manner that seemed to go through me, body and soul. I could feel the impression, like a wave of electricity, going through and through me. Indeed it seemed to come in waves of liquid love, for I could not express it in any other way. It seemed like the very breath of God. I can remember distinctly that it seemed to fan me, like immense wings.

No words can express the wonderful love that was shed abroad in my heart. I wept aloud with joy and love. I literally bellowed out the unspeakable overflow of my heart. These waves came over me, and over me, and over me, one after the other, until I remember crying out, 'I shall die if these waves continue to pass over me.' I said, 'Lord, I cannot bear any more,' yet I had no fear of death.

Late in the evening a member of my choir—for I was the leader of the choir—came into the office to see me. He was a member of the church. He found me in this state of loud weeping, and said to me, 'Mr Finney, what's wrong with you?' I could not answer for some time. He then said, 'Are you in pain?'

I gathered myself up as best I could, and replied, 'No, but so happy that I cannot live.'

He turned and left the office, and in a few minutes returned with one of the elders of the church, whose shop was nearly across the way from our office. This elder was a very serious man and in my presence had been very watchful. I had scarcely ever seen him laugh. When he came in I was very much in the state in which I was when the young man went out to call him. He asked me how I felt and I began to tell him. Instead of saying anything he fell into a most spasmodic laughter. It seemed as if it was impossible for him to keep from laughing from the very bottom of his heart.[86]

Finney went on to spearhead a revival in America which his biographer claimed 'literally altered the course of history'. Over half a million people were converted under his ministry, in an age when there were no voice amplifiers or mass communications. Billy Graham wrote, 'Through his Spirit-filled ministry, uncounted thousands came to know Christ in the nineteenth century, resulting in one of the greatest periods of revival in the history of America.'[87]

In communities where he preached, bars and saloons closed for lack of business and the crime rate dropped. Thousands of lives were changed by the message of the gospel, proclaimed by a man anointed by the Spirit of God.

As we look around today this is what we desperately need. We see broken people, a church in need of restoration and a society in need of transformation. We need revival, and for that we need to be anointed by the power of the Holy Spirit. Only when his people are filled with 'the Spirit of the Lord' will they be equipped for revival. The source of revival is the Holy Spirit who was poured out on the Day of Pentecost. That is why, as Martyn Lloyd-Jones (who preached a series of twenty-four sermons on revival in 1959 to mark the centenary of the great 1959 revival) said: 'Every revival . . . is really a repetition of what happened on the day of Pentecost.'[88]

The nineteenth-century American evangelist D. L. Moody said in one of his last sermons: 'See how He [the Holy Spirit] came on the day of Pentecost! It is not carnal to pray that He may come again and that the place may be shaken. I believe that Pentecost was but a specimen day.'[89]

The nineteenth-century Baptist C. H. Spurgeon, one of the greatest preachers of his day, planted churches in many different parts of London. Each time he climbed into the pulpit, Spurgeon could be heard saying, 'I believe in the Holy Spirit. I believe in the Holy Spirit. I believe in the Holy Spirit.' This is how he prayed:

O God, send us the Holy Ghost! Give us both the breath of spiritual life and the fire of unconquerable zeal. O Thou art our God, answer us by fire, we pray Thee! Answer us both by wind and fire, and then we shall see Thee to be God indeed. The kingdom comes not, and the work is flagging. Oh, that Thou wouldst send the wind and the fire! Thou wilt do this when we are all of one accord, all believing, all expecting, all prepared by prayer.

Lord, bring us to this waiting state! God, send us a season of glorious disorder. Oh, for a sweep of the wind that will set the seas in motion, and make our ironclad brethren now lying so quietly at anchor, to roll from stem to stern! Oh, for the fire to fall again—fire which shall affect the most stolid! Oh, that such fire might first sit upon the disciples, and then fall on all around! O God, Thou art ready to work with us today even as Thou didst then. Stay not, we beseech Thee, but work at once.

Break down every barrier that hinders the incoming of Thy might! Give us now both hearts of flame and tongues of fire to preach Thy reconciling word, for Jesus' sake! Amen![90]

10

How Should We Pray for Revival?
Isaiah 62:1–7

I have only been to the Wimbledon tennis champion-
ships once and I watched an up-and-coming seven-
teen-year-old called Bjorn Borg. Three years later he
won the Men's Singles. He went on to win forty-one
singles matches in succession at Wimbledon and the
most Men's Singles titles since the challenge round
was abolished in 1922—five consecutively between
1976 and 1980. In 1983 he announced his retirement
from professional tennis, but a few years ago he came
out of retirement and tried to return to the professional
circuit. At first he played with an old-fashioned
wooden racket and then with a modern racket. He
hardly won a game. Although only in his late thirties,
his ability to play tennis had sharply declined.

The sight of a sportsperson, or perhaps a business
in decline, pales into insignificance beside the tragedy
of a nation in decline. The best example in history is
probably the decline and fall of the Roman Empire,
but our society is also in decline, as divorce, violent
crime, sexual abuse of children, AIDS, drug abuse,
debt and alcoholism increase.

Isaiah 62 was written against a similar background. The prophet is heart-broken at the condition

of Jerusalem. He says, 'For Zion's sake I will not keep silent, for Jerusalem's sake I will not remain quiet' (Is 62:1a).

The word 'Zion' is used 152 times in the Old Testament as a title for Jerusalem (forty-six times in Isaiah). The name is a poetic and prophetic designation, with emotional and religious overtones. Jerusalem was both the royal city and the city of the temple, and Mount Zion was the place where Yahweh, the God of Israel, dwelt symbolically (see Isaiah 8:18; Psalm 74:2). The prophet says that because of the state of Zion he will not 'keep silent', but he will pray. For Jerusalem's sake he will not 'remain quiet'. The word used here means 'to be still, inactive'. He commits himself to ceaseless prayer and action for revival.

In the autumn of 1857, New York was in the midst of what was regarded as a national disaster—a financial crash which ruined many of its 1 million population. On 1 July, Jeremiah Lanphier, a middle-aged businessman, took up an appointment as a missionary in the city centre. Churches were suffering from depletion of membership as people moved out of town. Lanphier decided to start a lunchtime prayer meeting. On the first week, he prayed alone for half an hour until five others joined him. The following week twenty came. Within six months, 10,000 people came daily to pray and a revival in North America had begun. Samuel Prime comments, 'The places of prayer multiplied because men were moved to prayer. They wished to pray. They felt impelled, by some unseen power, to pray.'[91]

John Kilpatrick is Pastor of the Brownsville Assembly of God Church in Pensacola, Florida. As we have seen, *The New York Times* described what is happening there as 'the largest and longest Pentecostal revival in

America in almost a century'. In the introduction to his book, *When the Heavens Are Brass—Keys to Genuine Revival*, John Kilpatrick begins:

> Corporate businessmen in expensive suits kneel and weep uncontrollably as they repent of secret sins. Drug addicts and prostitutes fall to the floor on their faces beside them, to lie prostrate before God as they confess Jesus as Lord for the first time in their lives. Reserved elderly women and weary young mothers dance unashamedly before the Lord with joy. They have been forgiven.
>
> I see these scenes replayed week after week, and service after service. Each time, I realise that in a very real way, they are the fruit of a seven-year journey in prayer, and of two and a half years of fervent corporate intercession by the church family I pastor at Brownsville Assembly of God in Pensacola, Florida.
>
> The souls who come to Christ, repenting and confessing their sin, the marriages that are restored, the many people who are freed from bondage that has long held them captive—these are the marks of revival and the trophies of God's glory ... How? Only God knows. Why? First, because it is God's good pleasure, and second, perhaps because the soil of our hearts was prepared in prayer long before revival descended on us so suddenly.[92]

In June 1995, the visiting evangelist Steve Hill had preached a sermon which 'didn't seem to ignite any sparks'. But 'then he gave an altar call and suddenly God visited our congregation in a way we had never experienced before. A thousand people came forward for prayer after his message. That was almost half of our congregation! We didn't know it then, but our lives were about to change in a way we could never have imagined.'[93]

John Kilpatrick goes on: 'Revival will not come until God's people allow themselves to be changed and prepared through the discipline of fervent prayer.'[94]

What should we pray for? (vv. 1–5)

For Zion's sake I will not keep silent, for Jerusalem's sake I will not remain quiet, till her righteousness shines out like the dawn, her salvation like a blazing torch. The nations will see your righteousness, and all kings your glory; you will be called by a new name that the mouth of the Lord will bestow. You will be a crown of splendour in the Lord's hand, a royal diadem in the hand of your God. No longer will they call you Deserted, or name your land Desolate. But you will be called Hephzibah, and your land Beulah; for the Lord will take delight in you, and your land will be married. As a young man marries a maiden, so will your sons marry you; as a bridegroom rejoices over his bride, so will your God rejoice over you.

First, the prophet prays for a new righteousness. He longs for the righteousness of the city to shine out 'like the dawn' (v. 1b). Righteousness involves people living in right relationships with God and with one another. He is praying for the kind of righteousness we looked at in Chapter 7 when we examined Isaiah 58.

Recently I received a letter from someone who had been given an evangelistic booklet I have written. He said, 'On page one you write about the importance of relationships and I quote, "Christianity is first and foremost about relationships rather than rules. It's about a person more than a philosophy," and it occurred to me that if this is the case why is it that the Christian church has about as bad a track record on relationships as you will find anywhere? The church is split and divided into a multiplicity of groups and sects, and all too often there is considerable acrimony between those groupings . . . Nice little booklet, shame I have never seen its message as a reality in a group situation.'

Sadly, there is something in the point he makes. Over the centuries, the church has not been either as united or as righteous as it ought to have been. We need to pray for a transformation in the Christian church so that our 'righteousness shines out like the

dawn'—so that people see a Christian community which is united in love. True righteousness is tremendously attractive. From time to time, I have heard people remark as they start coming to a Christian church on the genuine love and practical help which they experience, but we must pray that this increases more and more, and that God continues to break down denominational barriers.

Secondly, he is praying for a new freedom—'her salvation like a blazing torch' (v. 1b). He prays that the fact that God has saved his people will shine out from the city. The word 'salvation' means 'freedom', release from bondage. This freedom was won for us by Jesus Christ (see Chapter 4; Isaiah 52:10—53:12). As people are set free by Jesus Christ from the bondage of sin they 'shine like stars in the universe' (Phil 2:15) or as Isaiah puts it here, 'like a blazing torch'. This will attract the attention of the world around, as 'the nations will see your righteousness, and all kings your glory' (v. 2a).

Thirdly, he is praying that God's people will have a new identity—'you will be called by a new name that the mouth of the Lord will bestow' (v. 2b). In the ancient near East, the giving of a new name to someone signified a radical change in their status and fortunes (eg the change of Jacob's name to 'Israel'). Instead of being known as 'deserted', they will be known as 'Hephzibah' which means 'my delight is in you'. Instead of being known as 'desolate' they will be known as 'Beulah' (which means 'married', v. 4). The image of the church today can often be one of a place that is deserted and desolate, irrelevant to modern life and with constantly dwindling numbers. Our prayer should be that it will be transformed into a place in which God clearly delights. The prophet is foretelling that the people of God 'will be a crown of splendour in the Lord's hands, a royal diadem in the hand of your God' (v. 3), that they will be guarded and upheld, possessing royal worth and dignity. The Lord's people will be a sign that he is King.

Fourthly, he is praying for a new love. He is longing to see Jerusalem as a bride, with God as the bridegroom. Verse 5a describes a wedding: 'As a young man marries a maiden, so will your sons marry you.' It is a picture of God committed to his people in a marriage covenant. The second half of the verse then depicts the honeymoon: 'As a bridegroom rejoices over his bride, so will your God rejoice over you' (v. 5b). Such will be the relationship between God and his people: a relationship of love that is genuinely experienced. It is a picture of commitment, love and joy. This is what we should be praying for in the church today.

"Apart from revival Lord, um, please - Cyril's snoring!..."

All this will happen when God comes to his people. The prophet prays later on: 'Oh, that you would rend the heavens and come down, that the mountains would tremble before you! As when fire sets twigs ablaze and causes water to boil, come down to make your name known to your enemies and cause the nations to quake before you!' (Is 64:1–2).

The invisibility of God has always been a problem for the people of God. The pagans laughed at them because they could not see their God, whereas they had statues that could be seen and touched. They mocked and said, 'Where is your God?' (see, for example, Psalm 42:3, 10). The psalmist asks, 'Why do the nations say, "Where is their God?"' (Ps 115:2). So the people cried out to God to come down and show himself.

Modern society asks similar questions. For instance, in the wake of the tragic school massacre in Dunblane in Scotland in 1996, *The People* carried the headline, 'Where was God at 9.30am on Wednesday, March 13th?'

God has dealt with this 'problem' of his invisibility supremely by revealing himself in the person of his Son. John says in the prologue to his gospel, 'No-one has ever seen God, but God the One and Only, who is at the Father's side, has made him known' (Jn 1:18). But also God has come down by his Spirit. In his first letter, John again opens the subject by saying: 'No-one has ever seen God' (1 Jn 4:12). But this time he ends in a slightly different way: 'If we love one another, God lives in us and his love is made complete in us. We know that we live in him and he in us, because he has given us of his Spirit' (1 Jn 4:12–13). God continues to make Jesus known and real to us by his Spirit.

The prayer which Isaiah prayed at the beginning of chapter 64, for God to 'rend the heavens and come down', is one which the church should still pray. The preacher Dr Martyn Lloyd-Jones writes in his book on revival, 'I do not hesitate to assert that that is the ultimate prayer in connection with a revival.' He relates one of George Whitefield's experiences while preaching at Cheltenham. Suddenly, during the sermon, 'God, the Lord, came down amongst us'. 'What does this mean?' asks Lloyd-Jones. He answers, 'It is a consciousness of the presence of God the Holy Spirit literally in the midst of the people ... God has come down amongst them and has filled the place and the people with a sense of his glorious presence.'[95]

Of the 1859 Irish revival, Tom Shaw said, 'It began when God moved upon the hearts of a small group of people, resulting in a prayer burden that never slackened until God rent the Heavens, and mountains of sin and evil flowed down at his presence.'[96]

There is no better way to pray for all this than to pray along the lines that Jesus taught us:

> Our Father in heaven,
> hallowed be your name,
> your kingdom come,
> your will be done
> on earth as it is in heaven (Mt 6:9–10).

Who should pray for revival? (v. 6a)

I have posted watchmen on your walls, O Jerusalem.

Watchmen had two different purposes in biblical times. First, they would look out for wild animals and thieves coming to take sheep and cattle. Secondly, they would be positioned within the defence works of larger cities, on the alert for hostile action against them. 'Watchman' was a term that came to be used of prophets and intercessors (Is 21:8–12). The Lord said to Ezekiel: 'Son of man, I have made you a watchman for the house of Israel; so hear the word I speak and give them warning from me' (Ezek 3:17). Jesus exhorted his disciples to 'keep watch' (Mt 24:42; 25:13), and to 'watch and pray . . . ' (Mt 26:41).

Just as all Christians are called to bear witness to Christ, but some have a special calling as 'evangelists', in the same way we are all called to hear the word of the Lord and to intercede for people, but some will have a special calling as 'intercessors'. The task of the watchman is to see and understand our current situation, in a way that is alert to possible attacks and problems as well as to what God wants to do, and to bring these strands together in prayer.

Not only are Christians to pray individually, but they are also to pray together for the Holy Spirit to revive the church. One of the best known promises in the Old Testament is the Lord's promise to Solomon that, 'If my people, who are called by my name, will humble themselves and pray and seek my face and turn from their wicked ways, then I will hear from heaven and will forgive their sins and will heal their land' (2 Chron 7:14). The 'healing of the land' is as good a definition of revival as one is likely to find. When we turn to the New Testament we see again that it is as God's people unite together in prayer that God acts. It was when 'they all joined together constantly in prayer' (Acts 1:14) that 'all of them were filled with the Holy Spirit' (Acts 2:4). The first Christians became a people 'saturated with God' and revival began.

C. H. Spurgeon wrote,

The Holy Spirit is sometimes represented as the wind, the life-giving breath. He blows on the valleys, filled up with the slaughtered, and they are brought to life. You and I, though we are made to live, often feel that life is flagging, and almost dying. The Spirit of God can bring us to life, revive in us the spark of divine life and strengthen in our hearts God's life. Pray for this quickening breath, and God will give it to you. As surely as you sincerely pray you will have and feel the revival of the life within.[97]

The revival that came to England in 1859, and particularly through the preaching of C. H. Spurgeon, can be traced back six years to the prayers of his London congregation. Spurgeon himself commented:

When I came to New Park Street Chapel it was but a mere handful of people to whom I first preached, yet I could never forget how earnestly they prayed. Sometimes they seemed to plead as though they could really see the Angel of the Covenant present with them, and as if they must have a blessing from him. More than once we were all so awe-struck with the solemnity of the meeting that we sat silent for some moments while the Lord's Power appeared to overshadow us; and all I could do on such occasions was to pronounce the benediction, and say 'Dear friends, we have had the Spirit of God here very manifestly tonight; let us go home and take care not to lose his gracious influence.' Then down came the blessing; the house was filled with hearers and many souls were saved.[98]

In the last chapter we looked at the remarkable events of Billy Graham's visit to England in 1954. In his autobiography, Graham acknowledges that prayer was the key. Just before the mission, 800 men and women spent the entire night on their knees, praying together for the mission. Prayer groups all over the world were focusing their attention on London for those meetings, including 35,000 groups in India.

From time to time during the crusade, Billy Graham

and the organisers scheduled all-night prayer meetings in venues all over London. Writing a report for a magazine in the US, Paul Rees, who helped organise the mission, listed six factors that he believed contributed to the historic impact of the London mission. First on his list was 'the power of prayer'.[99]

The answer to the question, 'Who should pray for revival?' is that although God may call and equip certain people to be 'watchmen' or 'intercessors' specially gifted in prayer, we all have a responsibility to pray, both individually and corporately.

How should we pray for revival? (vv. 6b-7)

They will never be silent day or night. You who call on the Lord, give yourselves no rest, and give him no rest till he establishes Jerusalem and makes her the praise of the earth.

First, we are to pray constantly. The watchman 'will never be silent day or night' (v. 6a). We are to be different from Israel's watchmen of the past who 'lie around and dream, they love to sleep' (Is 56:10). Instead, we are to 'pray continually', as the New Testament encourages us (1 Thess 5:17). Paul wrote to the Christians in Rome and told them, 'Constantly I remember you in my prayers at all times' (Rom 1:9-10).

The source of the river of prayer which flows in the South Korean church today originates in the dedicated prayer among missionaries and South Korean church leaders at the turn of the century. The Pyongyang revival of 1907 began at a mass meeting in which thousands were caught up in a wave of the Spirit which swept over the entire Korean church. An eye witness account described it like this:

After a short sermon Dr. [Graham] Lee took charge of the meeting and called for prayers. So many began praying that Dr. Lee said, 'If you want to pray like that, all pray,' and the whole audience began to pray out loud, all together. The effect was indescribable. Not confusion, but a vast harmony of sound and spirit, a mingling together of souls moved by an irresistible impulse to prayer. It sounded to me like the falling of many waters, an ocean of prayer beating against God's throne . . .

As the prayer continued, a spirit of heaviness and sorrow came upon the audience. Over on one side, someone began to weep and, in a moment, the whole congregation was weeping . . .

Man after man would rise, confess his sin, break down and weep, and then throw himself to the floor and beat the floor with his fists in a perfect agony of conviction . . . Sometimes after a confession, the whole audience would break out in audible prayer and the effect . . . was something indescribable . . . And so the meeting went on until two o'clock a.m., with confession and weeping and praying.[100]

Dr Jashil Choi, mother-in-law of David Yonggi Cho, gave herself to praying for long periods on a mountain, sleeping in a tent for three years. Ever since a permanent building was erected in July 1974, prayer meetings have been held every day and attract large numbers of people. As the years have gone by, prayer mountain has grown to be a place where thousands of people go daily to fast and pray. A modern 10,000-seat auditorium has been added which is now too small to hold the crowds that come. Attendance varies, but normally at least 3,000 people are daily praying, fasting, worshipping and praising our holy and precious Lord. In this atmosphere of concentrated prayer, healings and miracles are a common occurrence.[101]

David Yonggi Cho writes, 'I am convinced that revival is possible anywhere people dedicate themselves to prayer . . . it has been historically true that prayer has been the key to every revival in the history of Christianity.'[102]

Secondly, our prayer should be disciplined. Those who call on the Lord are exhorted to 'give yourselves no rest' (Is 62:6), to pray regularly, day in and day out. This is not always easy.

John Arnott, the pastor in charge of the Toronto Airport church which has been at the centre of a remarkable move of God's Spirit, wrote of his struggle to maintain a disciplined prayer life:

In my own case, the struggle has been desperate and intense. There have been seasons of wonderful times 'in the closet' with my Heavenly Father, praying to him in secret and being rewarded by him openly. During such times, one feels that everything is working out for the good, and one wonders why we could ever be so foolish

as to not spend generous hours in communion with God. Then suddenly the cares of this life descend with such fury that the new-found prayer route is derailed once more, and the battle to regain it continues.[103]

Thirdly, we are to pray with urgency. Not only are we to give ourselves no rest but we are to 'give him no rest' (v. 7). We are called to be passionate and pressing. Jesus told his disciples a parable 'to show them that they should always pray and not give up' (Lk 18:1). Although the judge in the parable 'neither feared God nor cared about men' (v. 2), he gave a persistent widow justice because she kept on asking until he was concerned that she would wear him out—'I will see that she gets justice, so that she won't eventually wear me out with her coming!' (v. 5). Jesus comments: 'And will not God bring about justice for his chosen ones, who cry out to him day and night? Will he keep putting them off? I tell you, he will see that they get justice, and quickly' (vv. 7–8).

"Come on Lord, Come on please please please"

The persistent widow is a good model for us as we pray for revival because she challenges us to be honest about our present state and to ask God passionately for change. 'Only when we realise and admit our true condition will we long for revival. Praying for revival is not enough: we must long for it, and long for it intensely.'[104]

The historian of revivals, R. E. Davies, wrote: 'The most constant of all factors which appear in revivals is that of *urgent, persistent prayer.* This fact is acknowledged by all writers on the subject.'[105]

Fourthly, our prayer should be persevering. The watchmen are to pray 'till he establishes Jerusalem and makes her the praise of all the earth' (v. 7). They are to pray until the whole earth gives praise to the Lord. Duncan Campbell writes of the 1949 Hebrides revival:

> I believe this gracious movement of the Holy Spirit . . . began in a prayer burden; indeed there is no doubt about that. It began in a small group who were really burdened. They entered into a covenant with God that they would 'give him no rest until he made Jerusalem a praise in the earth'.

They waited. The months passed, and nothing happened, until one young man took up his Bible and read from Psalm 24: 'Who shall stand in his holy place? He that hath clean hands and a pure heart . . . He shall receive the blessing from the Lord.' The young man closed the Bible and, looking at his companions on their knees before God, he cried: 'Brethren, it is just so much humbug to be waiting thus night after night, month after month, if we ourselves are not right with God. I must ask myself—"Is my heart pure? Are my hands clean?"'

He asked God to reveal if his hands were clean and his heart was pure. As they waited on God his awesome presence swept the barn. These men came to understand that revival is always related to holiness. Three men were lying on the straw having fallen under the power of God. They were lifted out of the ordinary into the extraordinary. They knew that God had visited them and a power was let loose that shook the parish from its centre to its circumference. In a house four miles away from the barn, two sisters, one aged eighty-two and doubled-up with arthritis, and the other a blind eighty-four-year-old, had a vision of God. They saw the churches crowded, especially with young people. They had a 'glorious assurance that God was coming in revival power'.

Their minister sent for Duncan Campbell to come for a ten-day mission, but he was booked up until the following winter. The minister read Campbell's reply to the two old ladies. They said, 'That is what man hath said, but God hath said otherwise. Mr Campbell will be here in a fortnight.' His convention was cancelled and he arrived on the island and went to the parish church. The meeting began at 9pm and continued until 4am. There was a crowd of over 600 inside, with still more listening outside. No one could explain where they had come from. Strong men trembled in the presence of God, and many fell prostrate on the floor. Within ten minutes Campbell's voice could not be heard, as so many were crying out to God for mercy. The sound of singing had been replaced with a cry of penitence—'God be merciful to me, a sinner.' As people experienced the holiness of God, they committed themselves to seeking after him. The movement swept into the neighbouring parish. There was such a sense of God there that one businessman visiting the island said, 'When I stepped ashore I was suddenly conscious of God. God met with me and saved me.'

The challenge facing the church today is to pray for God to 'rend the heavens and come down' (Is 64:1), to give us 'a consciousness of the presence of God the Holy Spirit literally in the midst of the people'. We need a new righteousness, a new freedom, a new identity and a new love. It is easy to give up interceding and to grow despondent when we do not see instant results, but we need to pray constantly, calling on the Lord in a disciplined and urgent way 'till he establishes Jerusalem and makes her the praise of the earth'. Individual and corporate prayer are a vital part of preparation for revival which in turn leads to greater individual and corporate prayer. As Billy Graham once said, the three keys to revival are prayer, prayer, and prayer.

" Given the options as laid out by Billy Graham, we chose prayer as no. 1 "

11

Where Will It End?

Isaiah 65

Here in the West, many assume that history is aimless. They share the view of William Shakespeare's Macbeth:

> Life's but a walking shadow, a poor player,
> That struts and frets his hour upon the stage,
> And then is heard no more; it is a tale
> Told by an idiot, full of sound and fury,
> Signifying nothing.[106]

Marxism is confident of the meaning of history. The class struggle drives the human race onwards until the means of production falls into the control of the proletariat and so a kingdom of justice, peace and perfection will be established. We have seen the collapse of that hope in the past few years.

Many Eastern religions have a circular view of history. Reincarnation, which involves an endless cycle of birth and re-birth, is fundamental to Buddhism, Sikhism and Hinduism. In each life we have to suffer the consequences of our actions in a previous one. Followers of these religions spend much of their energy trying to improve their life for the next cycle.

The biblical view is that history is 'his story'. It is moving towards a climax. The struggle is not between classes but between good and evil. It will culminate with the ultimate triumph of good and of God. To quote Bishop Lesslie Newbigin once again: 'The Bible gives a unique interpretation of universal history— the whole history of everything from creation to the end of the world. Therefore it tells us the meaning of our own story.'

So far in Isaiah we have seen, among other things, the greatness of God, the extent of his plan, the love of God, his unique plan of salvation and his invitation to all to come. That invitation requires a response. Throughout the Bible we hear a call for a decision rather than a universalism that believes all will respond to the gospel in the end. In this chapter we see four differences between those who choose for God and those who choose against. We will look at each in turn.

Those who respond and those who do not (vv. 1–7)

'I revealed myself to those who did not ask for me; I was found by those who did not seek me. To a nation that did not call on my name, I said, "Here am I, here am I." All day long I have held out my hands to an obstinate people, who walk in ways not good, pursuing their own imaginations—a people who continually provoke me to my very face, offering sacrifices in gardens and burning incense on altars of brick; who sit among the graves and spend their nights keeping secret vigil; who eat the flesh of pigs, and whose pots hold broth of unclean meat; who say, "Keep away; don't come near me, for I am too sacred for you!" Such people are smoke in my nostrils, a fire that keeps burning all day. See, it stands written before me; I will

*not keep silent but will pay back in full; I will pay it back
into their laps—both your sins and the sins of your
fathers,' says the Lord. 'Because they burned sacrifices on
the mountains and defied me on the hills, I will measure
into their laps the full payment for their former deeds.'*

God longs for a response. In its original context, this
passage was probably an appeal to both the faithful
and the unfaithful in the Jewish community. The
apostle Paul, however, sees it as having a far wider
application. He sees verse 2 as applying to the Jewish nation (see Romans 10:21) and verse 1 as applying to the Gentiles (see Romans 10:20). God is trying
to reach all people. Like a father beckoning a child,
he holds out his hands to us and says, 'Here am I,
here am I.' In the same way Jesus invited everyone:
'Come to me' (see Matthew 11:28). Yet he also said
that one day he would say to some, 'I never knew
you. Away from me' (Mt 7:23). That will be the
verdict on those who respond with words only but
not in deeds, on those who 'walk in ways not good,
pursuing their own imaginations'. As the General
Confession in the *Book of Common Prayer* puts it,
'We have followed too much the devices and desires
of our own hearts.'

Having opened with a general indictment, the prophet moves to the specific charges. First, they were
involved in forbidden practices. They were 'offering
sacrifices in gardens and burning incense on altars of
brick'. This refers to the false cults, probably involving Canaanite fertility rites and sexual immorality.
Often, people think that it does not matter what you
believe so long as you are sincere. But here we learn
that the worship of any god apart from the Lord is
offensive to him.

Secondly, the people were involved in occult practices (v. 4a) ('occult' means 'secret', 'hidden'). That is
what the prophet means by those 'who sit among the
graves and spend their nights keeping secret vigil'.
'To sit among the graves' means to consult the dead.
This is expressly forbidden in the Bible (see Leviticus
19:31; Deuteronomy 18:10–12), and any attempt to
contact the dead through mediums or seances is not
an option for Christians.

Thirdly, they were disobeying God's word. They
were breaking their own dietary laws (v. 4b), which
are laid out in Leviticus 11 and Deuteronomy 14.
These ancient laws were designed to preserve the
holiness and separateness of God's people by declaring which foods were 'clean' and which were not. The
Israelite people were meant to be holy in every aspect
of their lives, because God is holy. Here, they were
deliberately flouting God's laws by making themselves 'unclean'.

Fourthly, they were guilty of spiritual pride and
arrogance. This attitude of 'Keep away; don't come
near me, for I am too sacred for you!' (v. 5) is similar
to that of the Pharisee who said, 'God, I thank you that
I am not like other men—robbers, evildoers, adul-
terers—or even like this tax collector' (Lk 18:11).
This type of attitude is condemned (see Matthew
23:13–36). God says, 'Such people are smoke in my
nostrils, a fire that keeps burning all day long.' This is
probably a play on the Hebrew word for 'nostrils',
which also means anger. Such an attitude of superi-
ority towards others is offensive to God.

It is not the case that all religions lead to the same
God. God says of such false religious practices, 'See, it
stands written before me; I will not keep silent but
will pay back in full; I will pay it back into their

laps—both your sins and the sins of your fathers.'
Judgement is coming on those who refuse to worship
the one true God.

However, the invitation is extended to all. God
longs for each of us to respond to him. But the prophet recognised that not all will do so and God's
judgement will fall on those who do not respond.

Those who seek and those who forsake (vv. 8–12)

*This is what the Lord says: 'As when juice is still found in
a cluster of grapes and men say, "Don't destroy it, there is
yet some good in it," so will I do on behalf of my servants;
I will not destroy them all. I will bring forth descendants
from Jacob, and from Judah those who will possess my
mountains; my chosen people will inherit them, and there
will my servants live. Sharon will become a pasture for
flocks, and the Valley of Achor a resting place for herds, for
my people who seek me.*

*'But as for you who forsake the Lord and forget my holy
mountain, who spread a table for Fortune and fill bowls of
mixed wine for Destiny, I will destine you for the sword,
and you will all bend down for the slaughter; for I called
but you did not answer, I spoke but you did not listen. You
did evil in my sight and chose what displeases me.'*

A farmer in the Middle East about to chop down a
vine might suddenly see a cluster of grapes and
decide not to destroy it. So the Lord says there is a
remnant—'my servants'—whom he will not destroy.
More than that, he will bless them so much that the
Desert of Sharon, a plain in the western part of Israel
and a picture of waste and deterioration, will become
a 'pasture for flocks'. The Valley of Achor, on the east
side, also known as the Valley of Trouble, was the

place were Achan was stoned to death (see Joshua 7:24–26) and was a symbol of good being marred. It will become 'a resting place for herds'. Even in this valley there will be peace. This is a picture of God's blessing on the remnant who seek God.

The division was not so much between good and bad, but between those who sought God and those who forsook him (v. 11). The 'forsakers' forgot God and sought someone or something else. In particular they sought two other gods. First, they sought 'Fortune', a Syrian deity worshipped by the Canaanites, and probably one of the Astral deities of fate. It does not follow from this that gambling in all its forms is intrinsically evil but clearly the dangers are great.

Timothy O'Brien always played the lottery. His habit was to buy five weeks' worth of tickets in advance for himself and a workmate and then to fill them out with the same sequence of numbers: 14, 17, 22, 24, 42 and 47.

Last Saturday, Mr. O'Brien did not watch the lottery draw live on the television. So he missed Anthea Turner and Gordon Kennedy riding a steam roundabout in Norfolk. He missed the usual run of previous winners popping the champagne corks and smiling the smiles of those whose lives have been changed irrevocably. And he also missed the fact that the numbers which popped out of the tombola were 14, 17, 22, 24, 42 and 47. It wasn't until the next morning, when he read his Sunday paper, that he found out he was on a course to riches. Until, that is, he checked his tickets and discovered they had run out the previous week, thus depriving him and his mate of a share in the £8m jackpot. Unable to face his friend with the news that his bureaucratic incompetence had deprived him of a life change, Mr O'Brien . . . went up to the attic, loaded up the .22 pistol he used at his local gun club and shot himself in the head.[107]

The same article carrying this story quotes one news-agent as saying, 'People have become obsessed [with the lottery]. For some of my customers it is all they seem to live for. They spend their last pennies on it every week.' 'Gamblers Anonymous report that increasing numbers of women have sought help because they are hooked.'[108] As the pursuit of money can lead to worshipping the god 'Mammon' so the danger of gambling is that it can lead to worshipping the god 'Fortune'.

The second god the unfaithful Israelites sought was 'Destiny' (v. 11). Perhaps the modern equivalent would be those who practise astrology or see their fate determined by the stars. It is a form of paganism which is common in England today.

Susan Leybourne, a 'white witch', has been appointed as the country's first pagan university chaplain. She gives talks and guidance to students at Leeds University in magic, rituals and worship. Ms Leybourne says, 'When young people come to university it's probably the first chance they have to take an active interest in the occult. . . . As a witch and a chaplain I'm there to give advice.' Students from the Leeds Occult Society asked the witch to become their chaplain. As a pagan priestess she is asked to help mark festivals such as Hallowe'en and the winter solstice, and to teach the worship of Cernunnos, the horned god.

The worship of other gods is offensive to the Lord. He says, 'I will destine you for the sword and you will all bend down for the slaughter; for I called but you did not answer, I spoke but you did not listen.

You did evil in my sight and chose what displeases me.' This is a solemn warning to those who forsake the Lord.

Those who serve God and those who do not (vv. 13–16)

Therefore this is what the Sovereign Lord says: 'My servants will eat, but you will go hungry; my servants will drink, but you will go thirsty; my servants will rejoice, but you will be put to shame. My servants will sing out of the joy of their hearts, but you will cry out from anguish of heart and wail in brokenness of spirit. You will leave your name to my chosen ones as a curse; the Sovereign Lord will put you to death, but to his servants he will give another name. Whoever invokes a blessing in the land will do so by the God of truth; he who takes an oath in the land will swear by the God of truth. For the past troubles will be forgotten and hidden from my eyes.'

Actions have consequences. The fate of the two groups set out separately earlier is brought together here. Those who serve other gods will go hungry and thirsty—a picture of non-fulfilment. They will be 'put to shame', a picture of disappointment. They will cry out from anguish of heart and wail in brokenness of spirit. Ultimately, 'the Sovereign Lord will put them to death' (v. 15).

His servants, on the other hand, will eat and drink. They will have every need met. They will 'sing out of the joy of their hearts' (v. 14). This depicts total emotional satisfaction, which can only be found in a relationship with God through Jesus Christ.

Malcolm Muggeridge wrote:

I may, I suppose, regard myself, or pass for being, a relatively successful man. People occasionally stare at me in the streets—that's fame. I can fairly easily earn enough to qualify for admission to the higher slopes of the Inland Revenue—that's success. Furnished with money and a little fame even the elderly, if they care to, may partake of trendy diversions—that's pleasure. It might happen once in a while that something I said or wrote was sufficiently heeded for me to persuade myself that it represented a serious impact on our time—that's fulfilment. Yet I say to you, and I beg you to believe me, multiply these tiny triumphs by a million, add them all together, and they are nothing—less than nothing, a positive impediment—measured against one draught of that living water Christ offers to the spiritually thirsty, irrespective of who or what they are. What, I ask myself, does life hold, what is there in the works of time, in the past, now and to come, which could possibly be put in the balance against the refreshment of drinking that water?[109]

Those who do not serve the Lord have a correspondingly terrible thirst.

These verses are similar to the ones where Jesus speaks of a separation between those who serve God and those who do not as like a shepherd who divides his sheep and goats (see Matthew 25:31–46). Again, there is no middle ground, no hybrid, no category of those who are unsure, undecided or don't know. The fate of the goats (representing those who do not serve God) is terrifying: they are cut off from God (v. 41) and destroyed. On the other hand, the sheep (those who do) are invited to enjoy the presence of the King (v. 34) and receive an inheritance prepared for them before the world began. The New Testament makes clear that the basis of this judgement will be how we have responded to Jesus (see, for example,

John 3:36) and the evidence of our faith is our love—
especially for other Christians (see 1 John 2:9–10), but
also for our enemies (see Matthew 5:43–47). We
deserve hell and cannot save ourselves, but Jesus
died for us, to enable us to be his servants and to
make heaven a reality.

Isaiah foresees that the servants of the Lord will
receive a new name (v. 15). There is a clue as to
what this new name will be in the next verse. They
will act by 'the God of truth'. Literally, this means the
God of Amen, the Hebrew word which means absolute reliability and certainty. The apostle Paul writes,
'No matter how many promises God has made, they
are "Yes" in Christ. And so through him, the "Amen"
is spoken by us to the glory of God' (2 Cor 1:20). John,
in the book of Revelation, makes it even more clear
that 'Amen' is a title for none other than Jesus Christ.
He is 'the Amen, the faithful and true witness, the
ruler of God's creation' (Rev 3:14).

As we have seen, the servants were originally
intended to be Israel. Ultimately, only one person
fulfilled God's intention and plan. Now the St
Andrew's cross opens out again and the servants
are the people of God who take on the name of that
one Man and are known today as Christians.

Those on their way to heaven and those on their way to hell (vv. 17–25)

*'Behold, I will create new heavens and a new earth. The
former things will not be remembered, nor will they come
to mind. But be glad and rejoice for ever in what I will
create, for I will create Jerusalem to be a delight and its
people a joy. I will rejoice over Jerusalem and take delight*

in my people; the sound of weeping and of crying will be heard in it no more.

'Never again will there be in it an infant who lives but a few days, or an old man who does not live out his years; he who dies at a hundred will be thought a mere youth; he who fails to reach a hundred will be considered accursed. They will build houses and dwell in them; they will plant vineyards and eat their fruit. No longer will they build houses and others live in them, or plant and others eat. For as the days of a tree, so will be the days of my people; my chosen ones will long enjoy the works of their hands. They will not toil in vain or bear children doomed to misfortune; for they will be a people blessed by the Lord, they and their descendants with them. Before they call I will answer; while they are still speaking I will hear. The wolf and the lamb will feed together, and the lion will eat straw like the ox, but dust will be the serpent's food. They will neither harm nor destroy on all my holy mountain,' says the Lord.

This chapter ends with a picture of the new heaven and the new earth. The next chapter ends with a picture of hell. The future for those who rebel against God is that 'their worm will not die, nor will their fire be quenched, and they will be loathsome to all mankind' (Is 66:24).

For those who accept the authority of the Bible, there may be some debate about the nature of hell (for example, whether it means eternal punishment or judgement and annihilation), but there is no doubt about its reality. Equally, there is no doubt about the reality of 'heaven'. In this section the prophet looks forward to 'new heavens and a new earth' (v. 17). He anticipates a time when 'the wolf and the lamb will feed together . . .' (v. 25). This is 'apocalyptic' writing, like Revelation 21:1, 2 Peter 3:13 and Isaiah 66:22, which foresees the unveiling of the future when, one day, the kingdom of God will be fully realised. Through it we get a picture of what the new heavens and the new earth will be like.

It is, of course, only a picture: we have difficulty in describing the new heavens and the new earth since we do not have the necessary language or the experience. As C. S. Lewis wrote:

> There is no need to be worried by facetious people who try to make the Christian hope of 'Heaven' ridiculous by saying they do not want 'to spend eternity playing harps'. The answer to such people is that if they cannot understand books written for grown-ups, they should not talk about them. All the scriptural imagery . . . is, of course, a merely symbolical attempt to express the inexpressible.[110]

First there will be a renewed earth together with a renewed heaven. It is not only people who will be new creations, but creation itself will be restored. In Genesis we see God's creation of the universe and in Revelation 21 we see his re-creation, where he says, 'I am making everything new' (Rev 21:5). God's intention, and our certain hope, is that this earth will not be thrown away but 'creation itself will be liberated from its bondage to decay' (Rom 8:21). God's kingdom will come in its fullness and his will will be done on earth as it is in heaven.

In the meantime, in this fallen world, we are able to build *for* the kingdom, in Tom Wright's phrase. 'Every God-directed and Spirit-inspired act of love, mercy, justice, creative beauty and healing is an advance sign that God's kingdom is coming.'[111]

A famous violinist was due to play in a European

concert hall. On the advertisements an over-zealous publicity agent announced that the violinist would play on his Stradivarius violin, which was worth a fortune. He came on to the stage and played a superb violin concerto. Then he took his violin, put it on the floor and jumped on it. He smashed it to smithereens. The audience gasped. Then he said, 'I bought that violin at a junk shop on my way here. Now', he said, 'I will play on my Stradivarius.' In other words, he was saying, 'I can use even a violin like that and play superbly.'

Likewise, if God can do all that he is doing with a fallen world, we can scarcely imagine what he can do with a new heaven and a new earth.

There will be joy and rejoicing (vv. 18–19a). 'No eye has seen, no ear has heard, no mind has conceived what God has prepared for those who love him' (1 Cor 2:9). Heaven will be a place of incredible joy and laughter. Martin Luther once said, 'If you're not allowed to laugh in heaven, I don't want to go there.'

There will also be no more suffering and '. . . the sound of weeping and of crying will be heard in it no more' (v. 19b). This prefigures some of the last chapters in the New Testament: 'He will wipe every tear from their eyes. There will be no more death or mourning or crying or pain, for the old order of things has passed away' (Rev 21:4). There will be no need for hospitals or medicine. There will be no need for disaster relief. For the created world itself will be healed.

Everyone will reach their full potential (v. 20). This is a reversal of the curse pronounced on Adam and Eve for their sin and of God's declaration of shortening of life in Genesis 6:3. Premature death will no longer exist. 'Never again will there be in it an infant who lives but a few days, or an old man who does not live out his years; he who dies at a hundred will be thought a mere youth; he who fails to reach a hundred will be considered accursed' (v. 20). The New Testament goes even further with Jesus' promise of eternal life. There will be no need for funerals, undertakers or cemeteries. God's people will be given immortality (1 Cor 15:53).

All activity will be a blessing: 'They will build houses and dwell in them; they will plant vineyards and eat their fruit. No longer will they build houses and others live in them, or plant and others eat. For as the days of a tree, so will be the days of my people;

my chosen ones will long enjoy the works of their hands. They will not toil in vain or bear children doomed to misfortune' (vv. 21–23a). There will be no more work in vain. There will be no more labour or toil. Rather there will be a restoration of the rule over creation for which we were created (see Genesis 1:26; Revelation 22:5). Again, this is a reversal of the curse in Genesis 2.

There will be a closeness of relationship with God: '. . . for they will be a people blessed by the Lord, they and their descendants with them. Before they call I will answer; while they are still speaking I will hear' (vv. 23b–24). There will be no more struggling in our relationship with God. There will be no more unanswered prayer. We will have an unimpaired vision of God and of Jesus. 'We know that when he [Jesus] appears, we shall be like him, for we shall see him as he is' (1 Jn 3:2). 'I did not see a temple in the city, because the Lord God Almighty and the Lamb are its temple. The city does not need the sun or the moon to shine on it, for the glory of God gives it light, and the Lamb is its lamp' (Rev 21:22–23).

Finally, there will be harmony and peace: '"The wolf and the lamb will feed together, and the lion will eat straw like the ox, but dust will be the serpent's food. They will neither harm nor destroy on all my holy mountain," says the Lord' (v. 25). All relationships will be restored—even down to those of the animal world. There will be a unity, a closeness and an intimacy in our relationships. Nature will be restored. It will be a place of stability, safety, security and peace. The kingdom of God will be fully established. Martin Luther wrote, 'I would not give up one moment of Heaven for all the joys and riches of the world, even if they lasted for thousands and thousands of years.'

God invites us, through the prophet, to come to him, respond to him, seek him and serve him, and all this will be ours . . . and it begins now. Revival gives us a glimpse of the future. It will reach its culmination when Jesus comes again to establish a new heaven and a new earth. This is the climax towards which history is moving. No revival will be complete until Jesus returns.

Revival involves the whole Trinity. Our confidence that revival is coming is based on the nature and character of 'the Sovereign Lord', 'the Holy One', 'the creator of the ends of the earth': God the Father, who promises that 'the glory of the Lord will be revealed, and all people will see it' (Is 40).

The central message of revival is Jesus Christ, the suffering servant of Isaiah 53: his life, death and resurrection. He was despised and rejected. He was pierced for our transgressions. The punishment that brought us peace was upon him. He bore the sin of many. God raised him to life again. He has been raised, lifted up and highly exalted. He is the one we proclaim. In the words of Raniero Cantalamessa, 'The point is Jesus Christ. Whenever the Holy Spirit comes in a new and fresh way upon the church, Jesus Christ comes alive. Jesus Christ is set at the centre.'

The source of revival is the third person of the Trinity: God the Holy Spirit. He is 'the Spirit of the Sovereign Lord' (Is 61). He anointed Jesus. He anoints his people today 'to preach good news to the poor', 'to bind up the broken-hearted, to proclaim freedom for the captives and release from darkness for the prisoners'. As Martyn Lloyd-Jones put it, 'Every revival . . . is really a repetition of what happened on the Day of Pentecost.'

At the heart of revival is the love of God, a love that flows between the persons of the Trinity and out towards the world and in particular the people of God. God has compassion on his people (Is 49—50). God's love for us is revealed primarily through Jesus Christ and is poured into our hearts by the Holy Spirit (Rom 5:5). Our response is to love him and to love our neighbour.

The instruments of revival are his servants. God intended Israel to be his servant (Is 49) but only Jesus was completely faithful. It is God's plan that the church, through the victory of Christ and the power of the Holy Spirit, can and should be his servants today. All ordinary people, as members of his church, have the potential to be used by God in revival.

His vision for the church is great. It is a worldwide one. We are told to 'Enlarge the place of your tent, stretch your tent curtains wide, do not hold back; lengthen your cords, strengthen your stakes. For you will spread out to the right and to the left' (Is 54). The vision for revival is to fulfil the mission that Jesus gave to the church to 'go and make disciples of all nations' (Mt 28:19).

As we go, we are to invite people to come to the feast (Is 55). Those who are thirsty, those 'who have no money' can come and 'delight in the richest of fare'. We are all invited to seek the Lord while he may be found. We need to turn from wicked ways and unrighteous thoughts. Repentance and revival go hand in hand. We need to turn to the Lord who has mercy on us and freely pardons. He does so because the suffering servant has been 'pierced for our transgressions'. The invitation involves turning from sin, putting our trust in him who died for us, rose again and is alive today. As we come to him, we come to the feast.

Our mission should be a holistic one (Is 59). Love for God needs to be combined with a genuine love for our neighbour. This will involve social action and social service. Revival should have a transforming effect on society.

Since revival is a sovereign work of God, we are utterly dependent on God. We need to cry out, 'Oh, that you would rend the heavens and come down' (Is 62, 64). We need to pray 'your kingdom come'. Our prayer should be constant, disciplined, urgent and persevering.

All the time we need to recognise that every person coming into a relationship with God, every reconciled family, every hungry mouth fed is only a foretaste of the future. Revival will not be complete until the rule and reign of God is complete in the new heaven and new earth (Is 65—66). This will come about when the resurrected Jesus returns to reign on earth for ever and ever. Then, the devil and all his works will be destroyed, and the sound of weeping will be heard no more. The wolf and the lamb will feed together. God will be all in all (1 Cor 15:28). The new exodus will have taken place: the exile will be over. The restoration will be complete. Every hope and promise of revival will be fulfilled.

'Now is the time of God's favour, now is the day of salvation,' writes Paul, quoting Isaiah 49:8 (2 Cor 6:2). Now is the time to cry out to God, 'Oh that you would rend the heavens and come down.' Now is the time to proclaim the good news about Jesus in the power of the Spirit. Now is the time to bind up the broken-hearted, to set the captives free, to feed the hungry and to bring justice to the oppressed. Now is the time to repent, believe and come to the feast.

'Now these three remain: faith, hope and love,' wrote Paul in 1 Corinthians 13. 'But the greatest of these is love.' Now is the time to love, for God is love. Revival stems from his love: revealed to us in Christ Jesus, filling our hearts through the Holy Spirit, sending us out to bring his love to the world. The heart of revival is love.

Notes

1. Colin Whittaker, *Great Revivals* (Marshalls, 1984), p. 138.
2. *Asia Week*, 17 August 1994, p. 34.
3. *The Guardian*, 16 April 1994.
4. Ed Silvoso, *That None Should Perish* (Regal Books, 1994), p. 36.
5. C. Peter Wagner, *Spiritual Power and Church Growth* (Hodder & Stoughton, 1986), p. 57.
6. Miguel Uchoa, writing in *Anglicans for Renewal*, Summer 1997, p. 17.
7. *The New York Times*, 27 May 1997, p. A1 by Rick Bragg.
8. Solomon Stoddard, from the chapter 'The Benefit of the Gospel' in *The Efficacy of the Fear of Hell, to Restrain Men from Sin* (Boston, 1713), quoted by Michael J. Crawford, *Seasons of Grace: Colonial New England's Revival Tradition in Its British Context* (New York: Oxford University Press, 1991), p. 110.
9. See for example, the Introduction to Iain Murray's *Revival and Revivalism, The Making and Marring of American Evangelicalism, 1750–1858* (Banner of Truth, 1994), pp. xvii–xxii.
10. Brian H. Edwards, *Revival! A People Saturated with God* (Evangelical Press, 1990), p. 26.
11. John Stott, *The Message of Acts* (IVP, 1990), p. 61.
12. Robert E. Coleman, writing in *Tears of Revival* (eds Tim Beougher and Lyle Dorsett, Kingsway, 1995), p. 104.

13. John F. Sawyer, *The Fifth Gospel—Isaiah and the History of Christianity* (Cambridge University Press, 1996), p. 17.

14. The writer is either Isaiah himself, preaching a sermon to be read 150 years later, or someone writing in the tradition of Isaiah in the new situation. There is a difference of opinion between commentators as to whether Isaiah was written by one person, or by two or three different people. For our purposes, it is not of great importance. What is undisputed is that the context of the message is the exile.

15. Data taken from *Social Trends 26*, 1996 Edition. Central Statistical Office.

16. The Very Revd Dr N. T. Wright speaking at the Oxford Inter-Collegiate Christian Union (May 1993). (See also *The New Testament and the People of God* (SPCK, 1992) pp. 268–272 and *Jesus and the Victory of God* (SPCK, 1996).)

17. *The Guardian*, 7 February 1997.

18. *The Church Times*, 7 February 1997.

19. Jonathan Edwards, *The Works of Jonathan Edwards, Vol II* (Banner of Truth, 1992), p. 267.

20. William Blake, *Auguries of Innocence*, stanza 1 (c. 1803).

21. Everett L. Fullam, speaking at Holy Trinity Brompton (c. 1985).

22. Arthur Wallis, *In the Day of Thy Power* (Christian Literature Crusade, 1956), p. xi.

23. Malcolm Muggeridge, *Conversion* (Collins, 1988), p. 135.

24. Alec Motyer, *The Prophecy of Isaiah* (Inter-Varsity Press, 1993), p. 391.

25. *Ibid.*, p. 391.

26. W. M. Thompson, *The Land and the Book* (London, 1890), p. 203.

27. *Sports Illustrated*, 30 December 1996.

28. Eifion Evans, *Daniel Rowland and the Great Evangelical Awakening in Wales* (Banner of Truth, 1985), p. 53.

29. Jonathan Edwards, *The Works of Jonathan Edwards, Vol I* (Banner of Truth, 1834), p. lxv.

30. Eifion Evans, *op. cit.*, p. 314.

31. Raniero Cantalamessa, *Life in the Lordship of Christ* (Sheed and Ward, 1990), pp. 3–4.

32. Jonathan Edwards, *op. cit. Vol I*, p. 268.

33. Helen Shapiro, *Walking Back to Happiness* (Fount, 1993), p. 277.

34. Joachim Jeremias, *Eucharistic Words of Jesus* (SCM Press, 1996), p. 228.

35. Simon Weston, *Walking Tall: An Autobiography* (Bloomsbury, 1989), p. 144f.

36. Paul Yonggi Cho, *Solving Life's Problems* (Logos International, 1980), pp. 135–6.

37. Some critics suggest that the correlation between Isaiah's prophecies and the New Testament accounts is not a question of accurate foreknowledge but of the New Testament writers simply writing their accounts in a way which corresponded to Old Testament prophecy. There are occasions in the New Testament when the writer makes clear that he is making a link between his account and Old Testament prophecy (usually by citing verses from the prophets), but this does not require so sceptical a view.

38. Ian Barclay, *The Facts of the Matter* (Falcon Books, 1971), pp. 33–34.

39. *Daily Meditations for May 1996—The Spirit of Pentecost* (The Word Among Us), pp. 20–21.

40. Jonathan Edwards, *op. cit. Vol I*, p. 266.

41. Samuel Prime, *The Power of Prayer* (Banner of Truth, 1991), p. 11.

42. D. Martyn Lloyd-Jones, *Revival* (Marshall Pickering, 1986), p. 47

43. Timothy George, *Faithful Witness: The Life and Mission of William Carey* (InterVarsity Press, 1991), pp. 31–32.

44. C. Peter Wagner, *Scripture and Church Growth* (Hodder & Stoughton, 1986), pp. 55–56.

45. The Lausanne Covenant, from *Let the Earth Hear His Voice* (World Wide Publications), 4, p. 25.

46. Lesslie Newbigin, *Household of God* (SCM, 1952), p. 144.

47. *Ibid.*, p. 146.

48. Billy Graham, *Just As I Am: The Autobiography of Billy Graham* (HarperCollins, 1997), p. 696.
49. Osservatore Romano, 14 May 1990, pp. 4, 10.
50. Billy Graham, *op. cit.*
51. Jonathan Edwards, *The Works of Jonathan Edwards, Vol I* (Banner of Truth, 1992), p. 348.
52. John Pollock, *John Wesley* (Hodder & Stoughton, 1989), p. 172.
53. Arthur Wallis, *In the Day of Thy Power* (Christian Literature Crusade, 1959), p. 26.
54. Osservatore Romano, 18 September 1989, p. 4.
55. Alexander Solzhenitsyn, Templeton Address (Guildhall London), 10 May 1983.
56. C. S. Lewis, *The Weight of Glory* (in *Screwtape Proposes a Toast*, Fontana, 1965), p. 98.
57. Billy Graham, *op. cit.*, p. 697.
58. Tim Beougher and Lyle Dorsett, *Tears of Revival* (Kingsway, 1995), p. 15
59. Arthur Wallis, *op. cit.*, p. xi.
60. Jonathan Edwards, *The Works of Jonathan Edwards, Vol II* (Banner of Truth, 1992), p. 267.
61. Billy Graham, *op. cit.*, pp. 681–683.
62. J. D. Smart, *History and Theology in Second Isaiah* (Epworth, 1965), p. 247.
63. Nelson Mandela, *Long Walk to Freedom* (Abacus, 1995), p. 620.
64. *Ibid.*, p. 680.
65. *Ibid.*, p. 394.
66. James Gregory, *Goodbye Bafana Nelson Mandela My Prisoner, My Friend* (Headline, 1995).
67. Mary Benson, reviewing Mandela's book in *The Daily Telegraph*.
68. Nelson Mandela, *op. cit.*, p. 583.
69. *Ibid.*, p. 616.
70. Claus Westermann, *Isaiah 40–66* (SCM Press Ltd, 1969), p. 338.
71. K. S. Latourette, *A History of Christianity* (Payne and Spottiswoode, 1954), p. 1055.

72. Brian H. Edwards, *Revival! A People Saturated with God* (Evangelical Press, 1990), p. 193.

73. Bishop Lesslie Newbigin, *The Open Secret* (SPCK, 1995), p. 19.

74. Charles G. Finney, 23rd lecture on Revival.

75. George Carey, *The Church in the Market Place* (Kingsway, 1995), pp. 13–16.

76. From the Septuagint (the Greek translation of the Old Testament text).

77. D. M. Phillips, *Evan Roberts, The Great Welsh Revivalist and His Work* (Evangelical Press of Wales, 1923), p. 70.

78. Mark Edwards, *The Sunday Times*, 7 May 1995.

79. International Tree Foundation, *Trees Are Life* brochure.

80. These incidents in Billy Graham's life are taken from John Pollock's *Billy Graham: The Authorised Biography* (Hodder & Stoughton, 1996); William Martin's biography *The Billy Graham Story: A Prophet With Honour* (Hutchinson, 1991); and Billy Graham's autobiography *Just As I Am* (HarperCollins, 1997). The account I have given is a combination of these sources.

81. Frederick Booth-Tucker, *General William Booth* (New York Press, 1898), p. 105.

82. Samuel Prime, *The Power of Prayer* (Banner of Truth, 1991), p. 11.

83. Jonathan Edwards, *The Works of Jonathan Edwards, Vol I* (Banner of Truth, 1884), p. ix.

84. *George Whitefield Journal* (Banner of Truth, 1960), p. 201.

85. John Pollock, *George Whitefield and the Great Awakening* (Lion, 1972), pp. 147–9.

86. Lewis A. Drummond, *Charles Grandison Finney and the Birth of Modern Evangelism* (London, 1983) and *The Autobiography of Charles G. Finney*, condensed and edited by Helen Wessel (Bethany House Publishers, 1977), pp. 21–22. Helen Wessel has condensed the memoirs of the Revd Charles G. Finney, originally published in 1876, and updated many of the anti-

quated terms, shortened the sentences and modernised the punctuation.

87. Iain H. Murray, *Revival and Revivalism: The Making and Marring of American Evangelicalism 1750–1858* (Banner of Truth, 1994), p. 298.

88. D. Martyn Lloyd-Jones, *Revival* (Marshall Pickering, 1986), pp. 199–200.

89. R. E. Davies, *I Will Pour Out My Spirit: A History and Theology of Revivals and Evangelical Awakenings* (Monarch, 1992), p. 17.

90. Quoted in Arthur Wallis, *In the Day of Thy Power* (Christian Literature Crusade, 1956), p. 249.

91. Samuel Prime, *op. cit.*, p. 11.

92. John Kilpatrick, *When the Heavens Are Brass—Keys to Genuine Revival* (Revival Press, 1997), p. ix.

93. *Ibid.*, p. x.

94. *Ibid.*, p. xi.

95. D. Martyn Lloyd-Jones, *Revival* (Marshall Pickering, 1986), pp. 305–6.

96. Bob Dunnett, *Let God Arise* (Marshall Pickering, 1990), p. 75.

97. Robert Backhouse (ed.), *Spurgeon on Revival* (Kingsway, 1996), p. 93.

98. Brian H. Edwards, *Revival! A People Saturated with God* (Evangelical Press, 1990), p. 78.

99. Billy Graham, *Just As I Am: The Autobiography of Billy Graham* (HarperCollins, 1997), pp. 219–223.

100. Donald N. Clark, *Christianity in Modern Korea* (University Press of America, 1986), p. 8.

101. Paul Yonggi Cho, *Prayer, Key to Revival* (Word, 1984), p. 97.

102. *Ibid.*, p. 7.

103. From the preface of *Pray With Fire*, Guy Chevreau (Marshall Pickering, 1995), p. ix.

104. Brian H. Edwards, *Revival! A People Saturated with God* (Evangelical Press, 1990), p. 74.

105. R. E. Davies, *I Will Pour Out My Spirit* (Monarch, 1992), p. 217.

106. William Shakespeare, *Macbeth*, Act V, scene 5, lines 24–28.
107. *The Independent*, 12 April 1995.
108. *Ibid.*
109. Malcolm Muggeridge, *Jesus Rediscovered* (Collins, Fontana Books, 1969), pp. 99–100.
110. C. S. Lewis, *Mere Christianity* (Collins, Fount, 1952), p. 119.
111. For further reading on this subject, see N. T. Wright, *Following Jesus* (SPCK, 1994), chapters 6 and 12.

STUDY GUIDE

by

David Stone

The Revd Dr David Stone has devised the following questions to help you get to the heart of what Nicky Gumbel has written and challenge you to apply what you learn to your own life. The questions can be used by individuals or by small groups meeting together.

1. What Is Revival?

1. Why is it so important to stress that 'revival involves more than personal renewal'?
2. What is special about the book of Isaiah?

'. . . despite being written hundreds of years before Jesus' birth, these passages are exciting, encouraging and relevant for us today.'

---

3. What are the historical circumstances which gave rise to Isaiah 40–66? What parallels are there with our situation today?
4. In what ways is the word 'exile' an appropriate one to use of people in modern Western society?

2. Is Revival Coming? (Isaiah 40)

1. Can you identify the four messages proclaimed at the beginning of chapter 40?
2. List the different images which are used to describe God in these verses. How do you respond to these various pictures?

'Deep down, consciously or unconsciously, we all long to experience the presence of God.'

---

3. What 'ultimately unsatisfactory substitutes' do people build their lives on? What secure alternative does the prophet suggest? How does this work out in practice?
4. How do we know what God is like? What are the five sources of such knowledge which Isaiah identifies?
5. What does it mean to affirm that God is a 'power-sharing God'? In what ways does he want to share his power with you?
6. What is the difference between an eagle and a turkey? Is this distinction helpful as you look at your own experience?

'We must respond to the urgent need to get the message of the gospel out to the world. God empowers us not just for quick sprints but to run the race with perseverance.'

---

7. Do you think of revival as something that God will bring about by himself in his own good time? Or as something which it is our responsibility to bring about? How do you think Isaiah would tackle this issue?

3. Whom Will God Use?
(Isaiah 49:1–7)

1. Why is it unlikely that the 'servant' in Isaiah's four 'servant songs' refers only to the nation of Israel? What alternatives have been proposed?
2. Nicky suggests that 'servant passages apply at three levels'. What does he mean? How does this apply to us?
3. What are the 'three main tasks' which serve as 'identifying marks of God's servants'?
4. In what ways are the 'sword' and the 'arrow' particularly appropriate images to describe the ways in which God equips his servants?

'. . . times of waiting are not times to waste, but to use to increase our understanding of God and our intimacy with him. Indeed, God may spend many years preparing us and training us for a particular moment.'

---

5. How can you 'make God visible'? Make your answer as practical as you can.
6. Nicky describes the biblical pattern for God's servants in terms of 'first, the promise, then the difficulties and finally the fulfilment'. How does your experience reflect this pattern?
7. What role do you have in the church's God-given task of taking his salvation to the ends of the earth?
8. How many Christians in the world are thought to be committed to praying every day for revival? Are you among them? Why?
9. 'We need to tell people the good news and warn them of

the dangers of rejecting God.' How exactly would you explain what the good news is? And what are the dangers of rejecting God?

'The gospel is public truth for the whole world.'

---

4. What Is at the Heart of Revival? (Isaiah 49:8–50:3)

1. How do you respond to the question, 'Do you find it easy to believe that God approves of you?'? What leads you to answer it in the way you do?
2. What is meant by the 'covenant' between God and his people Israel? How did God respond to the fact that they broke it? What does this show about him?
3. What do we know about shepherds in Palestine? In what ways is God like this?
4. 'Both good and bad experiences can be the raw material through which God works out his purposes in our lives.' In what ways have you found this to be true?
5. Have you ever felt abandoned by God? How does the prophet answer this dilemma?

'. . . it is impossible for God to forget his people: his love is even greater than a mother's for her baby.'

---

6. What experience have you had of the Holy Spirit's activity as the 'Spirit of sonship'?
7. How do you feel about the suggestion that God has 'tattooed' you onto his hands?
8. Have you ever been in a situation where you felt that God's power was not strong enough? How does the prophet answer this objection?
9. Do you ever feel that God's promises are just too wonderful for the likes of you and draw back because you feel you do not deserve them? What do you think Isaiah would say to this?
10. What features do the testimonies of revival

quoted by Nicky have in common? How does this affect your understanding of what revival is and how it comes about?

'At the heart of every revival is God's heart of love for his people.'

---

5. What Is the Message of Revival?
(Isaiah 52:13—53:12)

1. Why is Isaiah 53 so important for Christians?
2. In what ways does Jesus embody the contrasts shown in Isaiah 52:13–15?
3. *'With God, apparent failure may actually be success.'* Can you think of any other examples of this principle?
4. Why were the people of Israel unable to recognise Jesus as the Messiah? In what ways does this attitude still persist today?
5. What does Isaiah 53:4–6 reveal about the link between sin and suffering?
6. Turning to verses 7–9, what is 'extraordinary' about the accuracy of this prophecy?
7. How do you respond to the idea that Jesus' death was 'planned by the Almighty Sovereign God'?
8. In what ways was the death of Jesus on the cross a 'triumph'?
9. *'He did that for me; there is nothing that I cannot do for him.'* How does this apply to you in your relationship with Jesus Christ?
10. In the light of this chapter, what must happen before revival comes to an individual? Do you feel that this has happened to you? Would you like it to?

'It is the death and resurrection of Jesus Christ that makes revival possible.'

---

6. What Is the Vision? (Isaiah 54)

1. What strikes you about the story of William Carey?
2. '. . . *if the Lord wants to convert the heathen, he can do it without your help.*' Can you identify what is both true and false about this statement?
3. What illustration is used of Israel in Isaiah 54 and 55? What is the keynote of these chapters?
4. How do God's instructions to Israel apply to the church today? In what ways are you putting these into practice in your situation?
5. An understandable reaction to all this would be one of fear! On what basis, then, is the prophet able to say 'Do not be afraid'?

'We may have complete confidence because he promises that the past is utterly behind us.'

---

6. '*The temptation to go after other gods is an ever-present one.*' In what ways have you found this to be the case? Is there anything which you need to put right in this area?
7. What new picture surfaces in verses 11–17? What are the three particular promises of God to his people which it illustrates?
8. God is sovereign even when everything seems to be going wrong. What experiences have you had which highlight this truth?
9. Spend some time thinking and praying about William Carey's famous watchword: '*Expect great things from God and attempt great things for him.*' How are you going to put this into effect?

7. What Is the Invitation?
(Isaiah 55)

1. Isaiah sets out four reasons why we should respond to God's invitation to come to him. What are they?
2. Are you fully persuaded that 'material things do not satisfy'? How have you discovered this?

'The trouble with idols is that they do not deliver the life they promise.'

---

3. What is unusual about the 'shop-keeper' in verses 1–3a? Have you taken up his offer?
4. How do verses 3b–5 build on what God says at the beginning of the chapter?
5. Why do we need to make the most of the opportunities we have to respond to God's invitation? What opportunities are you aware of? Did you take them? If not, why?
6. What are the negative and positive sides to repentance which are highlighted in verses 6–9?

'No matter how far we have fallen, God will forgive us.'

---

7. How would you respond to someone who said that they could not think of anything they needed to repent of? And at the other end of the spectrum, what would you say to someone who claimed that they were too bad to be forgiven?
8. In what ways does God intend the lives of his servants to be fruitful? Does your vision of what this involves match Isaiah's? How does it work out in practice?

8. How Should Revival Affect Society?
(Isaiah 58)

1. What are the two dangers which Michael Cassidy suggests lay behind the involvement of Christians in the genocide which took place in Rwanda? Can you detect any signs of these dangers in your own attitudes?
2. What does Nicky mean by 'privatised religion'? What is wrong with it? How can we avoid it?

'. . . evangelism and social action are partners, and both are needed in every local church programme as a responsible expression of Christian love.'

---

3. What are the 'three types of wrong which need to be removed from society' which Isaiah identifies here? What can God's servants do to bring about the necessary changes?
4. Nicky cites abortion as a glaring example of injustice, inhumanity and inequality in our own society. In what ways can Christians be 'involved in the structures of our society at a local and national level' to fight on such issues?
5. What three areas of human need does the prophet highlight here? Why do you think that such needs still exist, some 2,500 years later?
6. How would you seek to encourage and help someone who felt overwhelmed by the scale of the problems in our world that need resolving?
7. Are you in danger of being 'socially sensitive' but 'domestically negligent'? Why is this issue so important?

8. What does God promise here to those who obey him? What do these things mean in practice?
9. Among these wonderful promises, there is a further warning. What can spoil an 'advanced social conscience and flourishing ministry with the poor'?
10. According to these verses, what does it really mean to 'keep the Sabbath'? Do you?
11. Looking back over this chapter as a whole, why is the combination of love for God and love for our neighbour essential for true revival?

'True and lasting revival not only changes human hearts, but also communities and institutions.'

---

9. What Is the Source of Revival?
(Isaiah 61:1–11)

1. What does Nicky mean when he says that 'with much Old Testament prophecy, we can see three levels of fulfilment'?
2. What are the three levels of fulfilment for Isaiah 61? Why is it important to understand this and not leap straight to its application for us today?
3. According to these verses, what does it mean to be 'anointed' by the Holy Spirit?
4. Verses 1–3 highlight the results of such anointing on the lives of needy individuals. What exactly does Isaiah mention? How does this compare with your understanding of what ministry is about?

'The long-term effect of the ministry of the Holy Spirit is not just to give us the authority to bless the people around us and see their lives turned around; it is to put them back on their feet and to empower them, in turn, to support others who are in need.'

---

5. 'Christians today may receive material and financial support from unexpected sources.' How does Nicky reach this conclusion? Can you think of any examples of what he means?
6. The revival of the people of God is not an end in itself. What is it intended to lead to? How does Isaiah express this?

10. How Should We Pray for Revival?
(Isaiah 62:1–7)

1. Why do you think Isaiah 'is heart-broken at the condition of Jerusalem'? Do you feel the same about the state of the church and the world today?
2. Isaiah identifies four qualities to pray for in the life of God's people. What are these? Why are they so important?

'The image of the church today can often be of a place that is deserted and desolate, irrelevant to modern life and with constantly dwindling numbers. Our prayer should be that it be transformed into a place in which God clearly delights.'

---

3. What does the term 'watchman' highlight about the role of the prophet and the intercessor in the life of the church? Does this aspect of ministry ring a bell with you? If so, how can you put it into practice?
4. What five guidelines for intercession does Isaiah set out here?
5. What has been identified as 'the ultimate prayer in connection with a revival'? Why? What do you think would happen in your situation if God were to answer such a prayer?
6. Why do you think it is such a struggle to maintain a disciplined prayer life? Why is it so important that we do so?
7. What is the relationship between revival and prayer?
8. Why is revival 'always related to holiness'? What would God say to you in response to the question 'Are my hands clean and is my heart pure?'?

11. Where Will It End? (Isaiah 65)

1. What specific charges does Isaiah bring against those who refuse to respond to God's invitation to come to him?
2. How do you respond to the statement that 'God's judgement will fall on those who do not respond'? How do you think God feels about this situation?
3. What significance is there in the place names mentioned in verse 10?
4. Isaiah identifies a group who forsake God and seek someone or something else instead. What do they choose? Why does this lead to destruction?
5. What contrasts does the prophet draw between those who are God's servants and those who forsake him? Why are these so stark?
6. What, according to Isaiah, will heaven be like? Are you looking forward to it?

'. . . if God can do all that he is doing with a fallen world, we can scarcely imagine what he can do with a new heaven and a new earth.'

Alpha

The Alpha course is a practical introduction to the Christian faith initiated by Holy Trinity Brompton in London, and now being run by thousands of churches throughout the UK as well as overseas.

For more information on Alpha, and details of tapes, videos and training manuals, contact the Alpha office, Holy Trinity Brompton on 0171-581 8255, or STL, PO Box 300, Kingstown Broadway, Carlisle, Cumbria CA3 0QS.

All the books are available from your local Christian bookshop, or through Kingsway Publications, Lottbridge Drove, Eastbourne, E. Sussex BN23 6NT (Freephone 0800 378446).

Alpha **Hotline** for telephone orders:
0345 581278 (all calls at local rate)

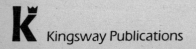

Kingsway Publications

Alpha

Alpha titles available

Why Jesus?   A booklet – given to all participants at the start of the Alpha course.

'The clearest, best illustrated and most challenging short presentation of Jesus that I know.' – Michael Green

Why Christmas?   The Christmas version of *Why Jesus?*

Questions of Life   The Alpha course in book form. In fifteen compelling chapters Nicky Gumbel points the way to an authentic Christianity which is exciting and relevant to today's world.

Searching Issues   The seven issues most often raised by participants on the Alpha course: suffering, other religions, sex before marriage, the New Age, homosexuality, science and Christianity, and the Trinity.

A Life Worth Living   What happens after Alpha? Based on the book of Philippians, this is an invaluable next step for those who have just completed the Alpha course, and for anyone eager to put their faith on a firm biblical footing.

Telling Others: The Alpha Initiative   The theological principles and the practical details of how courses are run. Each alternate chapter consists of a testimony of someone whose life has been changed by God through an Alpha course.

Challenging Lifestyle   Studies in the Sermon on the Mount showing how Jesus' teaching flies in the face of modern lifestyle and presents us with a radical alternative.

*All titles are by Nicky Gumbel, who is on the staff of
Holy Trinity Brompton*

——— ❖ ———